Whitworth College Library
0 0068 00013276 8

P9-DUF-551

New Theology No. 10

New Theology No. 10

Edited by
MARTIN E. MARTY
and DEAN G. PEERMAN

The Macmillan Company, New York, New York
Collier-Macmillan Publishers, London

The Macmillan Company
866 Third Avenue, New York, N.Y. 10022
Collier-Macmillan Canada Ltd., Toronto, Ontario

Library of Congress Catalog Card Number: 64-3132

First Printing 1973

Printed in the United States of America

Contents

Introduction: *Bios* and Theology

Bios = life. In the theological tradition rooted in the New Testament, three words in Greek are translated "life." One of these, *psyche*, is closer to our word "soul" in its connotations. That leaves *bios* and *zoe*. *Bios* is the rarer, less glamorous term. It appears only a half-dozen times, where it refers to the circumstances of organic life or the material resources for supporting it. The prodigal son wants his "living," and the widow gave of her "living." Man is "choked by the cares and riches and pleasures of *bios*." The "pride of *bios*" is a threat to man's life in God.

The Oxford English Dictionary introduces the English prefix "bio-" as having to do with "life, course or way of living" and connects it with a number of other words. The term also appears as part of an underused word, "biotic," which in the OED means "of or pertaining to (common) life, secular." More recent dictionaries are more neutral about the secular and content themselves with "having to do with life; live; vital." *New Theology No. 10* is preoccupied with the theme of *bios*. Were we given to neologisms, we would follow Dr. Van R. Potter, who coined "bioethics" in order to meet new necessities, and speak of "biotheology." No doubt some writers already use the term. Were we daring enough to try to rescue a nearly obsolete word, we could say this all deals with "biotic theology." But the "bio" section, significantly, is already one of the most rapidly expanding sections of the dictionary. Suffice it to say that theologians and ethicists today are doing what they can to come to terms with the manifestations of life, in all its changes.

What about *zoe*? *Zoe* refers to the more exciting dimensions of life in traditional theology. The Christian knows life as a result of the resurrection of Jesus Christ. He already participates in "eternal life." This kind of life is the dynamic, vivifying, exciting element in historic religious terminology. It transcends "(common) life, secular life." When theologians shift their metaphor from *zoe* to *bios*, the reader is alerted to the fact that something of significance is going on. There *is*.

In part, the shift is simply characteristic of a long-term trend in Western theology to come to terms with the natural order, with progress and process, atoms and molecules, the empirical and political worlds. The nineteenth-century German neo-Kantian theologians complained of "the acute Hellenization" of Christianity, which had been born Hebrew and thus was more at home in the world than it was after the fusion with Greek thought. Twentieth-century Roman Catholic philosophers often say that they are trying to remove the statues of Plato and Aristotle—which they claim have been the real icons—from the Catholic sanctuary. Theology, even a theology that seeks to speak of transcendence, has a this-worldly tinge and endeavors to speak to the common, secular life of man, to situate him in a world of things and effects.

From one point of view, this kind of theology can be seen as confining, limiting, inducing claustrophobia, suffocating. "All we've got is our bodies; let's take good care of them." Such thought takes the measure of the narrowing borders of human existence, the frailty of bodily life, the need for man to affirm in the midst of temporality and the physical. Then it affirms. This kind of thinking has gone into about half of the presuppositions of the theology in *New Theology Nos. 1–10*. As anthologists, reporters, and delineators, we have felt it important to present significant essays even if we are not wholly at home with them; and the editors have never been wholly at home with "secular" theology. It seems unimaginative, reductionistic, not always necessary for human self-understanding. It neglects many Christian resources and limits theological vision. We have, however, tried to do justice to its positive side, its desire to help man come to terms with, and to affirm his situation in, the concrete world.

Biotic thought deals not only with "common, secular life," but simply with living, vitality, and the like—according to the more recent dictionaries. In such circumstances, it need not be restricted to the confining. There is room for vitalist interpretations of transcendence. One moves into and through the created order and the life of man for signals of transcendence; where else are words, images, models, signs shaped? Theology with this accent is less confined and more ambitious. It is ready, in ever so modest ways, to talk about the *Logos*, the divine Word in the created order. Far from being less radical than secular theology, it asks for bigger investments in that order and demands more philosophical and experiential resources on the part of its practitioners. It can easily turn foolish, just as secular theology sometimes could. Neoreligious thinkers are often pressed to overadvertise every kind of magical, mysterious, mystical phenomenon or fad in culture. They make too much theologically of the anthropological and sociological models that include religious dimensions, but they represent creative counterparts to the "merely worldly" theology of the early 1960s.

When the theme for *New Theology* is introduced each year, it is necessary for the editors to say how they came to it. In a mechanical sense, the answer never varies. We are vocationally placed where it is necessary to observe not only year by year, but week by week, the productivity of people who write theology. We monitor periodicals and learned journals, attend conferences, interview theologians, use reporters' instincts to smoke out what it is that really agitates or quickens people. We consult friends on whose intuitions and learning we can depend. Then come the arduous days in libraries, where all the journals of the year past have to be explored to check out hunches. Some have seen in the decade's enterprise a kind of breathless sense of new discovery: throw your old theology away, here is the new model.

Those who read the introductions will find that this has not been the case at all. Of course, there is a passion for newness in the theological world, as elsewhere, for two reasons. First, there is no point in engaging in something unless one is alert to the implications of change. Secondly, the Christian tradition, to which we have most consistently turned, has newness built into its program and charter. "Behold, I make all things new!" Innovation has to be part of the vocabulary of theologians in a tradition that is born of "the new creation in Christ," but the devotion to the new does not mean that all has been repudiated from the past. If one needs proof that the editors have not so conceived their work or that the readers have not so apprehended it, they should be informed that the appearance of a new volume does not significantly cut into the circulation of earlier volumes. They stay "alive."

What we have noticed, however, is that *New Theology* has really meant two theologies through the ten years. They may be as old as Christian thought. They may perpetuate the traditions of Antioch and Alexandria, the cities whose schools provided options for early Christians. We have described them over-simply above and characteristically speak of them as secular or neoreligious and transcendental theological stirrings. They are both present in all the volumes, including this one.

When one has established these two lines of thought, the former a surprise to idealist and otherworldly Christians, the latter a surprise to "secular man," the task has been to seek the model or metaphor with which theologians have been working. That means the realization this year that for some time *bios* and its cognates and analogues and extensions have been a major preoccupation.

Selecting *bios* means neglecting other themes, and the journals and conferences have been full of these. The discipline of theology and religious studies is crowded and is growing ever more crowded. Academically situated, it is ever more specialized, advanced, and professional. That means that almost no one can afford to drop any subject or that someone will be dealing with every subject. But the treatment of many of these is tired, overworked—not a fit realm for *New Theology*.

The Congress of Learned Societies in the Field of Religion that was held in Los Angeles on September 1–5, 1972, provided opportunity for an assessment of the theological scene. Those attending were alerted to watch for signals, given two circumstances. On the one hand, academic religion has been an inflated, enlarged world. In the past ten years, the higher study of religion has been a growth industry—so much so that almost 3,000 international scholars could be gathered for this biggest-yet congress of its kind. On the other hand, theology and professional study of religion belongs to a strangely diminished world. Its presuppositions tend to be liberal and radical in a world that closes itself off in ever more intransigent conservatisms. It affirms the life of the mind while Jesus people and Pentecostalists celebrate the immediate experience. Most publishers who are interested in survival do not schedule long, "serious" theological tomes in their publishing lists. The market for jet set and celebrity theologians has turned downward since post-Vatican II Catholics and Protestant radicals offered so much promise and sensation in the mid-1950s.

The theological enterprise, therefore, presented something of the spectacle of so many fields of study in our day. Its practitioners seem often to be casting about aimlessly. Their craft improves, but there seems to be a sterility to so much of their specialized work. Not many observers could find how religious studies contributed to "the humanizing of man," as the tautologous conference theme advertised that they did. Activity, skill, ambition, expertise—these were abundantly evidenced at Los Angeles. But more often than one could wish, there was a sense of exhaustion; everything has been tried. In that respect, the theological world sometimes resembles the postradical political world of the 1970s: *anomie* afflicts many. There is a kind of joyless, directionless continuation of courses upon which one has embarked. Enthusiasm is left to the enthusiasts who cover up the emptiness of their lives by premature closure, who participate in pep rallies devoted to Jesus as the "one way."

So it was that we could not honestly report new vitality in biblical theology. As a movement it has, for now, had its moment. Biblical scholars are as expert as ever, but the life of "the people of God" is not being vivified by much of it. The history of religion is pursued phenomenologically—though one senses that not a few of the neoobjectivists who want to teach religion without getting involved are aware that their students do use them as priests and gurus, and their sources as sacred texts.

Systematic theology is the bearish part of the market. A new Evangelicalism is in the air in American church life: revivalism, evangelism, Pentecostalism, pietism all are having a new day; but little of this carries over into the world of interpretation and theological construction. There are evangelical theologians of note, but who in the culture needs to cope with their thought?

Neoorthodoxy remains eclipsed; its writings are now being exegeted by historical theologians, but are not chiefly used as revelatory for today's human situation. Mid-1960s-style radical theology left a legacy; it freed people from having to keep up appearances and pretenses. Positively and substantively, however, it projected little with which people have to reckon today; so it was not easy to key in to many of the theological movements of the century past.

At Los Angeles and elsewhere, however, it was possible to see that one area of theological thought was alive. It had been coming to life during the past years when we were collecting material on transcendence, politics, futurism, peoplehood—themes that have not been diminished significantly. "It" refers to the preoccupation with the paradigms related to *bios*.

How does one begin to recognize the signals? For the past several years, we have been not unaccustomed to picking up a telephone and hearing someone ask for suggestions for speakers or resource people. "We are having a seminar on. . . ." We can fill out the rest of the sentence: ". . . abortion . . ."—or euthanasia, health, medical ethics, aging, child development, artificial transplants of parts of the body, genetic tampering, and the like and the like and the like. Do we know of a Jewish or Christian theologian who can bring religious thought to bear?

Silence. Eventually, we mumble and stammer a few names. "Well, if you want a pretty direct affirmation of the changes in biological understanding, there's always Joseph Fletcher; you know him for the celebrity days of 'the new morality.' But long before that he was talking 'morals and medicine.' And if you want someone to say 'go slow for the sake of the human,' there is Paul Ramsey, who takes a rather negative view of things. And after that thesis/antithesis, how about James M. Gustafson for synthesis? His mediating position will help your conferees learn the range and complexity of issues. That's about it." Or we could move into the post-Catholic or Catholic orbits and recommend a Robert Francoeur or a Charles Curran or a John Dedek.

Had the questioner asked for people who could give theological or ethical interpretations of war and peace, race and poverty, almost any social metaphor or problem area, our list would have been lengthy. But for a long time, the demand far exceeded the supply in the world of biotic theology. That is changing. Cynics might say that theologians smell a fresh market area and scramble to it. That is not quite the case; the field is not all that dazzling. Preparation for it is arduous. The phonies can be spotted almost instantly; you see, in these dialogues there is really somebody out there who knows one half or one side of these things: medics, geneticists, or biologists can keep their counterparts honest. A better explanation: the topics are so urgent that men and women have had to begin to take on the difficult work of addressing the "bio-" subjects.

This volume interrupts them, not at midpassage, but

fairly early in the venture. Not many of them are ready to claim that they have mastered their subjects, that they really know how to interpret or what to tell others to be and do. They are pathbreakers, pioneers, venturesome folk who will permit themselves to be vulnerable.

Why the difficulty in speaking? Part of it stems from the complexity of all the subjects and the unforeseeable character of their futures. No one knows the future of politics, but Christians have lived with parliaments, elections, and revolutions for centuries. They have precedents for interpreting politics, but they have no precedents for interpreting organ transplantation or genetic experiment on any significant scale. They know the outcomes of revolutions and can make choices in the light of these. They and their scientific counterparts do not know the potential outcomes of many of their experiments.

For these reasons, it has been necessary to gather resource people. One illustration of this kind of gathering is the Institute of Society, Ethics and the Life Sciences (623 Warburton, Hastings-on-Hudson, New York 10706). The director, Daniel Callahan, sits with medics and theologians, is directed by a board that includes men such as Theodosius Dobzhansky, and is advised by a council that includes Karl Menninger. There and elsewhere, the beginnings are being made, and the results are coming out in books and in the kinds of journal articles reproduced here. Most of the attention to date has been given to "bioethics" and not theology or interpretation. The reason for that is simple to see: the changes are so urgent that one cannot wait for the perspective of the years and limitless research. One must act. But this action is its own kind of interpretation; and this ethics, whether or not it mentions God, is its own kind of theology.

Urgencies? Some of them need to be cited. The most dramatic instance has to do with the possibility that human nature itself can now be changed in the laboratory. In the immediate future, we are asked, can we expect the world scientific communities to practice permanent self-restraint, or will not someone somewhere begin a process that others shall pursue? For through *in vitro* fertilization or cloning it may begin to become possible to have asexual and, in a way, parentless reproduction of human beings, who will bear traits that their "creators" choose to give them. Tomorrow, "not born of woman"—a Shakespearean phrase—may apply, as Robert Francoeur likes to remind his readers, to a nine-month gestation in an artificial womb or in a subhuman surrogate mother; or the "it" may be the product of asexual cloning that bypasses egg, sperm, genital intercourse, fertilization, and pregnancy. It may be possible to reproduce the least (or most) aggressive human types, to breed in or screen out conflict and physical strength or artistic temperament, to shape optimists or pessimists.

The implications dwarf the set of questions associated with conventional ethical issues. Even atomic warfare did not represent such a qualitative leap. Men had been told that the age of space travel would drastically alter our interpretation of the universe and our theology. It hardly made a dent and required virtually no theological straining. However, the genetic alteration of human types—that is another question. The generation for which today's theology and ethics are being written is the one that, no doubt, will have to make decisions about the course taken.

The other ranges of issues in "bio-" styles of thinking are not much less dramatic, though some have begun to be lived with. Birth control is not as unsettling as it used to be, even in Catholic theological circles. Still, the presence of Pope Paul VI's encyclical *Humanae Vitae* and the debates it stirred or the rejections it inspired show something of the political and personal weight attached to the subject.

More plaguing is abortion, which is totally resisted as "murder" by a significant minority in the population and by a substantial number of theologians and which is simply and totally affirmed by many Women's Liberationist leaders, "new moralists," and, again, many ethical and theological thinkers. Most of the debate, however, has had to do with slogans: "Abortion on demand." "Abortion is feticide, and thus murder." Seldom is it theologically searching or capable of pushing further the inquiries concerning the initiation, nature, value, and intention of fetal life. Only beginnings have been made.

White House conferences on youth or the American Medical Association's Congress on the Quality of Life are indications of cultural openness to the discussion of values and ethics as they relate to pregnancy, birth, infancy, child development, and adolescence. Theologians are scurrying around, sometimes under the tutelage of an Erik Erikson, to have something to say about such developmentalism. Christian and Jewish theological resources are either meager or undeveloped on these subjects.

Health and healing come to be major preoccupations of a this-worldly technological and affluent society, wherein people can afford medical research and sophisticated practice to prolong biological life and make the human organism healthier and more comfortable. But with these come choices, as deans of any medical school in the country can underscore. Whereas a few years ago the medical ethos often seemed to be designed studiously to avoid ethical questions, today the students demand concentration on the issues having to do with the meaning of their vocation. Religion has always been connected with healing; witch doctors in the primitive religious world, Christ the healer in Christianity, the promise of good life and days in Judaism—these are typical. But they now appear on a new scale and in different and newly demanding contexts.

One side of conventional modern theological topics has to do with *bios*. Political and revolutionary theology deals, as Paul Ricoeur reminds us, not only with institutions and values, but also with goods—remember, *bios* meant also the material resources for living. Ecology, very near the center of much recent religious thought, locates man in nature and inspires debates about environment and human organism, man in control of nature and man in nature, and hence his "life" and his "living." Christian biopolitics—to use Kenneth Cauthen's term—links ecological and political concerns.

Still another area that has to be noted in a discussion of *bios* is the whole drug culture, particularly in its serious medical dimensions. David P. Young speaks of *A New World in the Morning: A Biopsychological Revolution* and points to others who have studied "mood drugs": Donald B. Louria, John Kaplan, and others. He also refers to ESB, electronic stimulation of the brain, a field in which José M. R. Delgado, who is represented in this volume, is the pioneer. (*Physical Control of the Mind: Toward a Psychocivilized Society* is his well-known book.)

The bio-logical and theological dimensions of the encounter culture are also obvious. Here we refer to the cluster of intensive group experiences that were clumped by Thomas Oden under the category "The New Pietism." Sam Keen calls marathons, sensory awareness experiences, enounter groups, T-groups, and Esalen-experiments a "soft revolution," a "new secular religion": it is eclectic, experiential, mystical, and nonprofessional—a do-it-yourself kit composed of disciplines and insights drawn from many religious and occult traditions. Affirmation of the body and bodily experience is at the heart of many of these phenomena. So much is this so that Thomas Hanna can speak of *Bodies in Revolt* and deal with a "somatic" or bodily revolution, which was inspired by Darwin, Freud, Lorenz (and other ethologists), Piaget, Reich, or—on other levels—by Kant, Kierkegaard, Marx, Cassirer, Camus, Merleau-Ponty, and Nietzsche. Theology, particularly that inspired by phenomenology, reckons with this somatic revolution, only one of whose dimensions is the whole sexual revolution that has so preoccupied ethicists in recent years.

Aging comes near the end of the cycle derived from *bios*. Simone de Beauvoir's extremely gloomy *Coming of Age* was a major indicator of the attention being given the subject by philosophers. Elizabeth Kübler-Ross in her death-and-dying seminars was typical of those who attracted ministers and theologians to an astonishingly taboo subject in the modern world. The minister who asked a Sun City dowager why she played bridge, danced, played shuffleboard, but would take part in no causes, was told, "I just want to keep the ever-livin' juices flowing." She was expressive of one side of the somatic revolution as it relates to aging and death, however pathetically she symbolizes it all.

Some of those who talk about *bios* have even begun to concentrate again on *zoe* and on eternal life. Debates about immortality and resurrection will no doubt be recast in the light of fresh concepts of life, living, and body; but they are present.

The biblical and Jewish or Christian traditions have resources for beginning work on these subjects. The Old Testament literature on man and his environment is much more complex than scientist-philosopher Lynn White would allow in his attack on Genesis' man-in-control mandate. Man is not only to subdue or dominate the physical world, he is also to live in and with it in wonder—and Hebrew Scriptures never tire of reminding him of this. Christianity is also, as William Temple put it, "the most material of all religions." The Epistle to the Hebrews says that the divine-human drama is played out not "out there," but in the middle of nature and history, in the Incarnation. Jesus' concern for the bodily needs of people led him to help them break religious (Sabbath) laws for the sake of food, led him to become a feeder and a healer; sacramental theology is very material in its affirmation of water and bread and wine.

To say, however, that there are resources is not to say that there will not have to be reconceptions. Many of the major theological schools of our time wrestle with concepts of God as Creator in the light of the revolution having to do with *bios*. Currently dominant are evolutionary and process-directed schools of thought inspired by Pierre Teilhard de Chardin, Alfred North Whitehead, and others. Man comes somehow to be "cocreator" or at least coresponsible for creation. Jesus Christ is pictured in Paul's Epistle to the Colossians as the one for whom and in whom and through whom the cosmos was created, and in him "all things hold together." This cosmic Christ is then pictured as "the first fruit of the New Creation," directing man back into the world with care for earth, community, person—and "life" itself—as part of the mandate. The witness to the Holy Spirit comes up in renewed theological debates over freedom and order and determinism; notice the debates inspired by Jacques Monod's *Chance and Necessity* and B. F. Skinner's *Beyond Freedom and Dignity*.

Christian theology can bring a negative, go-slow note to the proceedings. Bio-logical preoccupations can serve to be part of technological tampering, depersonalizing, dehumanizing. Thus the prophetic and almost dour Jacques Ellul warns that "when technique enters into every area of life, including the human, it ceases to be external to man and becomes his very substance. It is no longer face to face with man but is integrated with him, and it progressively absorbs him" (*The Technological Society* [Vintage, 1964], p. 11). Over against this, it also has the go-ahead view of Karl Rahner, the Continent's most prestigious Catholic theologian: "Freedom enables man to determine himself irrevocably to be for all eternity what he himself has chosen to make himself." And again: "There is no reason why man should not do whatever he is really able to do. A truly alert morality would, therefore, attempt to show contemporary man that what he ought not to do is, even today, impracticable. This holds true even on the historical, this-worldly level, where he may think it is possible to go against his moral duty."

The debate over fabricated man, technologized man, man-in-control, the new image of man, is heating up. Theologians are chartered to speak *coram deo*, in the sight of and in range of the experience of God. We have been impressed by the thoughtfulness of many of the pioneers. Few of them have panicked or shrieked or cried "Wolf!" in the face of bio-logical change. Most of them have quietly and patiently undertaken difficult tasks with some imagination. Our hope is that while trying to do justice to *bios*, they will ever be alert to those dimensions implied also by the reference to "the more abundant life," *zoe*.

The plot of *New Theology No. 10* is very simple, since most of it has been provided by the simple chronology of *bios*, the sequence from nonlife through life to death. But simple plots sometimes need complex introductions; so this anthology opens with three theoretical pieces, designed to guide the reader into the intricacies of the later essays and into subsequent inquiries concerning the subject. From a theological point of view, almost everything talked about in this book relates to the concepts or doctrines of creation and nature. So it is that Robert T. Osborn's article on a Christian view of creation for a scientific age properly leads off. Osborn is impressed by the opening that Heisenberg's principle of indeterminacy provides for thought about creation. It is "a symbol of man, and a call to man to fill the void and the indeterminant not with God and supernatural notions, but with man and scientific discovery."

The focus on indeterminacy and human discovery is not to everyone's taste; the German theologian Wolfhart Pannenberg begins at a much different point. Drawing on resources in both Paul Tillich's and Pierre Teilhard de Chardin's views on spirit and life, he discusses "self-transcendence" and relates it to creative processes. A much different alternative appears in Van Rensselaer Potter's discussion of "the ethics of nature and nurture"; here is the humanist approach, carefully outlined by the man who certainly deserves inclusion in this book since, among other things, he coined the now-familiar word "bioethics."

Ordinarily, bibliographical essays are tucked into the back of books, but Father Richard A. McCormick's essay on the moral literature having to do with genetic medicine is such a helpful delineation of the various positions that we deemed it a good introductory piece for the bulk of the book. Among the authors introduced by McCormick is Paul Ramsey, truly a pioneer among Christian theologians who have been preoccupied with the genetic questions. Ramsey wrote for the medical profession in an article that studiously set out to avoid explicit theological reference. But Ramsey can never refrain from being at least implicitly theological, and those who approach this book with exclusively theological interests will find his theme to the point.

Whereas Ramsey, for the moment, bracketed theological concerns, William Vrasdonk is explicit about them in his article on eugenics. He is not alone in referring to Paul Tillich as a frontier commentator on the subject. Although Vrasdonk allows for drastic human intervention in the evolutionary process through what is sometimes called "genetic tampering," he also suggests that the tendency of religious thinkers to urge scientists to refrain from some experiments is a well-intended and creative "don't."

Perhaps the most controversial topic in the field—at least until the public becomes fully aware of the implications of genetic experiment—is abortion. Rachel Conrad Wahlberg's defense of women's choice in the matter of abortion was a prizewinning essay, a clear statement of one option. The next article, Sister M. Romanus Penrose's "Virginity and the Cosmic Christ," may impress some readers as being an eccentric and almost irresponsible choice. If they read closely, however, they will see that the author, drawing on Teilhard and resorting to language that many will regard as "mythical," makes a contribution to the discussion of evolution as well as to that having to do with "the spiritualization of love."

Rachel Conrad Wahlberg's article should alert those who have not yet been alerted to the fact that in the discussions of *bios* and life-processes, the voices and concerns of slightly more than half of the human race will be heeded. Daphne Nash relates the liberation of women to trends in Christian marriage. She argues that if married Christians can help find alternatives to the nuclear family and link these alternatives to radical politics, Christian marriage can itself be experienced as "the scandal and revolutionary critique of society that it should be."

New Theology No. 10 seeks to be a contribution to the dialogue between theologians and humanists, and José M. R. Delgado's article on brain manipulation returns to humanist argument—in this case, the article is lifted from the pages of *The Humanist*; so no one is sailing under false colors. By no means all humanists will agree with Dr. Delgado's proposals concerning a strategy for mental planning, but he is the most influential spokesman for a point of view that is gaining adherents, and should be listened to, no matter what choice others make concerning it.

The sequence of earthly lives ends with death. Today death and dying have become newly problematic subjects; Daniel Maguire turns his attention to death as process, not as moment. He believes a healthier attitude toward death would emerge from more open discussion. For the Christian, death does not have the last word; the Lord of death and dying, the Lord of the resurrection, pronounces that "life is the absolute." Speaking in that Christian context, James M. Sullivan closes out this decade of new theological writing with a simple but dramatic meditation penned at the death-camp city of Dachau, Germany. "The journey to Life is routed through the heart of humanity and an acceptance of certain death." We guess we should add: "Amen!"

M. E. M. and D. G. P.

I. Creation and Nature

A Christian View of Creation for a Scientific Age

Robert T. Osborn

To contend that the doctrine of creation is a symbolization of faith—"a statement about God 'verified' in man" and one that is "not in competition with scientific cosmology"—is not to beg questions, in the opinion of Robert T. Osborn; "it is the only way the biblical tradition allows us to speak and . . . it is a viable way of looking at man in relation to the creation." Examining the doctrine of creation as theology, as anthropology, and as cosmology, Dr. Osborn concludes that religion is "the friend of science as science, the enemy of science as religion." A professor in Duke University's Department of Religion, Dr. Osborn has published articles in a variety of journals and is the author of *Freedom in Modern Theology*. His present article was first published in the Spring 1972 issue of *Religion in Life*.*

The Christian concept of creation is a doctrine of faith; i.e., it is a matter of faith and revelation (or intuition, if you will) and not one of scientific discovery. "By faith we understand that the world was created by the word of God." (Heb. 11:3.) Furthermore, as I understand it, the doctrine of creation is first of all a statement about God and not nature; secondarily it is a statement about man; and then, because man is in the world, also a statement about the world. Above all it is a theological statement, then anthropological, and finally cosmological.

About verification. Inasmuch as the doctrine of creation

* 201 Eighth Ave. South, Nashville, Tenn. 37202.

is concerned primarily with God and his creativity rather than with the world as creature, its subject matter is in a sense a priori and not subject to the principles of verification appropriate to science. Yet there is a type of theological verification, a historical type, which has to do with the degree to which faith in the Creator makes sense out of and to this extent verifies existence. It is not a question of proving God and the event of creation, but rather of providing an honest, authentic, and realistic negotiation of life and history. Ian Ramsey designates this type of verification an "empirical fit"—the ability of the creation faith to "incorporate the most diverse phenomena not inconsistently."[1] Ramsey's point is not that a theological model, such as the picture of God as creator, provides a theoretical synthesis or world view which explains and unites all the diverse elements of the world, but that it does lead to a way of life which acknowledges realistically all the elements of life and courageously negotiates them. Such a life may be designated as authentic or true. The verification of a theological model is achieved, therefore, not by establishing the correspondence between the model and its object, but by demonstrating the power of the model to establish a corresponding spiritual subject. As I stated at the outset, the doctrine of creation is first of all a statement of faith in God, secondly a statement about man. We can see now that it is a statement about God "verified" in man. It is not in competition with scientific cosmology. I hope to show that such a view is not a begging of questions but that it is the only way the biblical tradition allows us to speak and that it is a viable way of looking at man in relation to the creation.

The Doctrine of Creation as Theology

As we have seen, the doctrine of creation is first of all an affirmation of faith in God—God as creator. It is not a consequence of reasoning or inference from a firm empirical base or premise. Descartes was certain in his conviction that he existed, and on this premise alleged to have proved that God exists. Modern man, perhaps not so certain about himself as was Descartes, does, however, seem certain of the reality of the world about him, and should he be interested in God tends to establish his existence in scientific or empirical terms. The Christian is not certain of either of these starting points; he is not sure that in reason or in the material world man as man or God as God really appears or can be proved to exist. He finds no certain beginning point, and a God who is inferred from either stance is no more certain and divine than the premise. Kant showed that reasoning from the world to God could not reach to God simply because it could not escape the world. Stated a bit differently, the issue is not the salvation of God by man certain and secure in himself and his world, but rather the salvation of man and his world by God who certainly is. Only God can announce and authenticate his existence—and this he has done, says faith (not experience or reason), in Jesus Christ, above all. And in this announcement he reveals himself as creator.

Creation faith is a statement about God authorized by God himself. In his coming to Israel and in his presence in Jesus he announces first that he is, secondly that he is not alone, and thirdly that he is with the cosmos as its beginning and end. The logic of Israel's experience with God insofar as it speaks of creation comes to intuitive and symbolic expression in Genesis 1 and 2. I say intuitive and symbolic because it pierces beyond the world of mind and sense to its divine origins in a way that is properly described as intuitive. It is symbolic because it speaks of the Creator and the event of creation in terms of the creature. In scientific terms we might say that these stories are models.[2] Because the Christian believes the last word is spoken in Jesus, the Genesis account must be read by him in light of this final word. Such a reading is implicit in this article.

The first word of Genesis is that God is: "In the beginning God." Biblical history begins not with Abraham but with God, who calls Abraham (Gen. 12:11). That God is, that God is God before he is creator and redeemer, is the meaning of the biblical doctrine of election. Creation and redemption are elections of God; they are not necessities of the divine being, for God *is* before he creates. The New Testament doctrine of grace makes the same point; God creates in a gracious overflow of his being and not out of an inner, divine need.

Genesis 1 says also that God is not alone, that his being in himself is not at odds with his being with something other than himself. Christian theology, which affirms God's being for another in a most radical way in its doctrine of the incarnation, points to the congeniality of the divine being for this relationship in its doctrine of the Trinity, which denotes the eternal, relational nature of the Godhead. That God is not alone and that he can in consistency with himself tolerate another is symbolized when Genesis 1 tells us that in six days God created a reality outside himself.

The God of Israel not only appeared to earth but remained with it, in a preeminent way, as he went with Israel. Christianity believes that ultimately God so identified himself with his creation that he became one with man. In the language of Genesis, just as God created the world in six days' time, so he took the seventh of the days of creation for himself to be with the creation. God's is the last day. He is not only the alpha but also the omega of the creation; not only its once-for-all creator but also its continual provider.

Is this rather objective, symbolic talk about God meaningful? I remind you of my beginning—the uncertainty of the Christian about his own existence, whether it be viewed rationally or empirically; his uncertainty that reason or nature brings to him his true being. The only alternative he knows to this doubt and possible despair is the word of God and faith—the certainty that God is, that he created the world, and that he is for and with the world. It is only because God is that the Christian is certain about whatever else is—himself and his world. Because of theology there can be anthropology. He is like a man in love who cannot meaningfully call life without love real life. He will not be dissuaded in his judgments by suggestions that his loving point of view is merely that—a point of view, subjective and with no cognitive or ontological worth. No, life without love is not life; man and world without God in no real sense are.

The Doctrine of Creation as Anthropology

The biblical doctrine of creation insofar as it is more than theology is primarily anthropology.[3] John Dillenberger rightly observes that modern existentialist Christianity, which puts man, in his concrete, personal existence, at the center of theological concern, is the most biblical form of Christianity since the Reformation.[4] God revealed himself as creator by the creating of men—Abraham, Isaac, Jacob, and Joseph—a people, a new nation under God. He revealed himself by people to people, by going with them and by manifesting himself to them in their election, preservation, and direction. And for the Christian the last word of God is spoken when he becomes a person and completes the holy, redemptive history by the exaltation of an individual, personal man. The centrality of man in the creation narrative is symbolized by his creation on the "sixth" day as the *terminus ad quem* of the first five days of creation. He is created in the image of God. He stands on two feet, of and above the world—of the world in the sense of being a creature from dust to dust except as sustained by God's word and power; and above the world inasmuch as the world looks to man for its own meaning and fulfillment. In this relative superiority and authority over the world man is an image of God. Genesis 1 also explicitly refers to human sexual existence as an image of God, suggesting that, like God, man cannot find his being in his relationship to the world but only in relationship to his own kind, and that this relationship between man and man, especially that between man and woman, has a depth and aspects which are quite analogous to the relationship between God and man into which God calls man. As the creature of the sixth day man stands —to have dominion over the earth, to relate radically to his own kind, and to be in the image of God and qualified for relationship with God. The story, as we have noted, ends with God's rest on the sabbath within the time of man, signifying that while the *terminus ad quem* of the cosmos is man, the *terminus ad quem* of man is God. It is only in and from God that man is man, that he can stand above the earth without a vain and prideful denial of his feet of clay, and that he can stand on the earth without a lazy, indolent surrender of his stance above and his responsibility for it. Man is theocentric. He is not a materialist who finds his meaning in the world, nor is he an idealist who is himself the sovereign source of all meaning and reality. He is a God-man who in God finds his being and meaning so as to become a man and, as such, the source of being and meaning for the cosmos.

I would comment at this point briefly about the symbols of the trees in Genesis 2. The tree of life symbolizes that the being in the world given Adam is life—life indeed. The tree of knowledge of good and evil of which Adam was forbidden to eat symbolizes the fact that man's goodness and being cannot become his own responsibility; he is a creature and not his own creator. The command not to eat of this tree gives Adam the freedom to accept his being and goodness as a gift of God and take it up in his own freedom and decision. Now although Adam is not a responsible creator of himself, he is responsible for the world—to subdue it and to name its creatures. He does not name himself (nor God)—God does that. For himself and his good, God, not he, is responsible; for the world and its good, he is responsible.

The Doctrine of Creation as Cosmology

Because the Bible is concerned with man, it is concerned with the world—the world of nature, the object of scientific discovery and control. The error of traditional supernaturalism is in its naturalism, in its search for God in exceptional happenings of nature, whereas the God of the Bible is suprahistorical, manifest in exceptional historical events—like exodus and crucifixion. Nature is not the conveyer of God to man; rather man confers divinity upon nature. The issue theologically then is between God and man; only indirectly (insofar as it is concerned with man) is theology interested in nature. I would suggest, however, that there is a hierarchy which has epistemological relevance—God first, man second, and the world third. The relationship between God and man is the first relationship, the model for understanding that which exists between man and the world. As I said earlier, man is a created creator; as he is created, so he creates.

The relationship between the creator God and man the creature is one of freedom; it is a miraculous unity of sovereign divine intention and free, creative response, so that what comes to pass in each creative act of God is unique and new. I would suggest that there is a similar unity in freedom where man creatively encounters the world, so that the final product, the cosmos, is both a creature of man's active and expressive freedom and of the world's free response. As evidence I cite the role of the scientific model as explained by Ian Ramsey. It is a creature of imagination, insight, and intuition—a creature of human freedom—on the one hand, and the result of the free disclosure of nature on the other. It provides a creative insight into nature, bringing to view what as a matter of fact is not there apart from this unity of insight and disclosure. The world of scientific discovery is both from man and nature.

Obviously I must guard against two false monisms—one in which man the model-maker is viewed as the creator of the world *ex nihilo*, the other in which man the model-receiver is regarded as the *ex nihilo* product of nature's disclosure. I do not intend to say either that the world has nothing to say in the process of scientific discovery or that it has everything to say. If one approaches the relationship between man and nature on the model of that relationship which exists between God and man, then it should be understood that the original truth is that unity of man and nature in which man as such and nature as such are abstractions, yet in which man and nature are not identical or lost to the unity between them. But this relationship is ordered, so that just as man discovers and discloses himself only in answer to God, so also nature discloses and discovers itself (what it really in itself is) only in answer to man's creative word. When God spoke the word that created the world, he knew what he was doing and gave an original truth and reality to that world—a truth which is partly in the world and partly in man, and in its totality is disclosed and effective only as the world answers to man. In this sense man is co-creator with God (just as man is real and true in himself, but actual and effectively so only in answer to God).

Since nature is meant for man, the goal of scientific discovery (it is proper to speak of a goal of discovery inasmuch as it is an event of freedom, decision, and purpose) is the humanization of nature. However, since man is from God and for God, the meaning of humanization is not arbitrary or whimsical. The very fact of the world as a gift of God to man reveals its necessity for man. Therefore the discovery and control of the world will be with regard to its preservation and conservation (just as God's deification of man exalts rather than destroys man). Furthermore, since man is made for and with his fellow man, the discovery and development of nature will serve all men and their relationships (just as God's relationship to man is an expression and confirmation of his own triune nature). And, finally, because man is a creature of God's creative freedom, his own creativity will be an expression of freedom as manifest in his vision of beauty and order (just as God created man in his image). Freedom cannot be confused with license; it is not freedom to consume and destroy. In freedom man transcends nature with visions of beauty and order. Freedom which consumes and destroys is a false freedom—in fact, a slavery to the world manifest in a pathetic and destructive hunger for the earth rather than a creative freedom over it.

The humanization of the world is the goal of creativity. By humanization I mean the preservation and conservation of the world, its discovery and renewal for the good of men, and its transformation by the artistic vision and creative beautification. The world is humanized when it meets man in the unity of freedom; it depends upon man, upon his freedom and renewal.

To speak about the goal of scientific discovery and creativity is also to speak of the end—the *eschaton*. Eschatology, of course, has to do with the goal and end of all things and not merely scientific discovery. Science and technology are not the only expression of man's creativity; for he is also a social being, creatively ordering and renewing his world in political and ethical activity for instance, and humanizing it in the broad reaches of his cultural expression. In all his creativity he is moving toward the end. In the symbol of the resurrection he has the promise of victory and therefore the courage of his unfinished task. I would suggest that the resurrection with its vision of a bodily triumph contains all that the body implies—man's corporeal and spiritual nature and world. This symbol promises therefore not the deliverance of man from his world but the fulfillment of his task in the world in spite of the sin and death which threaten it. It promises, in the language of the Bible, "a new heaven and a new earth." It assures the Christian that God will win, that man will therefore prevail in his freedom, and that as man prevails so will the earth be delivered from its travail. That hope roots firmly in the faith born of resurrection, and in the meanwhile man, abiding in the love of God, continues in that love for the world by which the world itself will be saved.

Creation and Redemption

Let me state again that the doctrine of creation is a symbolization of *faith*; it is not descriptive but prescriptive. It is not meant to say what empirically is but what it is all about, and what, by the grace of God, it may actually become. Man and world as God's creatures are gifts of God; and since the world looks to man for its meaning, the first gift is the gift of selfhood to man. As Paul says, the creation groans in its travail awaiting the redemption of man. Empirically, man tends either to deny his creative responsibility or to forfeit it in a surrender to his own creatures. He, for example, wrests from the cosmos the secret of the atom, masters and smashes it, but at the same time is threatened by atomic destruction. This issue is man himself—his redemption and renewal in the image of God as free creator. Biblical religion witnesses to the action of the Creator in such a redemption that renews man in his humanity. It witnesses the salvation, exaltation, and in a sense the deification of man—his exodus from bondage, his exaltation in resurrection. If the freedom of man expressed in his creative intuition is of the essence of scientific discovery, then the renewal of man, the gift of freedom, and the restoration of the divine image is a calling to, and the empowering of, scientific and technological creativity. Religion is not threatened by science; religion is a patron of science. If religion brings God to man and, through man, God to the world, then science is not a problem for religion; what science knows about the world as such is not God; what divinity is in the world is there primarily because of man, and man is there because of God. Man himself is a threat to science when he surrenders his creative freedom; and science, not religion, is a threat to man when it becomes subject and man its object. Religion which is the renewal of man by God is therefore the friend of science as science, the enemy of science as religion.[5] Man, in the imagery of Genesis 3, is a fallen creature who continues to fall—to fall below the heights of creativity to which his creator calls, and who falls prey to the creatures of his own hand. Religion is redemption from fall and the exaltation and liberation of man the creature that he might become man the creator. It is a story of God become man that man might become like God—just a little lower than the angels.

I have argued that as a creature of God man is finished and good, but that, as a creator of the world, he is incomplete, and that therefore this incompleteness is of the essence of his divine and created nature. However, there is a sense in which man as creature of God is incomplete—insofar as he exists in sin, which by definition is not a dimension of his created self or of the created world, but which puts him into contradiction against his authentic self. Redemption thus involves, as it were, the completion of man himself (as opposed to the completion of his creative responsibility); yet this redemption is not so much a completion as a restoration of man to or renewal of man in his created and complete nature as God's son.

Creation, Redemption, and Science

These final remarks are only to make more explicit points already touched upon and to draw some conclusions. On theological grounds I have argued that the doctrine of creation is an affirmation of faith: first, that God is; second, that therefore man and the world are; and, finally, that as God is to man, so man is to the world—as creator to creature. The world as God's creation is in fundamental measure also a creation of man. When I turn to look at what some scientists and interpreters of science are saying, I find, somewhat to my surprise, that they are making a similar point. I have already cited Ramsey, in particular his discussion of the element of creativity—imagination, intuition, insight—in the construction of the scientific model. My contention that man is above nature and that his relation to God is the key to a creative relationship to nature is confirmed by Michael Polanyi when he states that he would speak first of the human person and then expand into an analysis of discovery. Self-discovery is most relevant for world discovery. If one is uncertain about himself, then he is inhibited in his discovery of the universe; he cannot proceed into the universe by escaping himself, for only through himself does he penetrate the universe. "There is no other way of approaching a hidden meaning than by entrusting ourselves to our intuitions of its yet unseen presence."[6] The extension of comprehension "involves an expansion of ourselves into a new dwelling place."[7] In a word, scientific knowledge, like the knowledge of other human beings, is personal.

Polanyi's thought is pioneering and exotic only in its analysis of this phenomenon of personal, scientific knowledge, not for its identification of the phenomenon. Bernard Morel also identifies the personal dimension when he states that "in man's technical and scientific effort he [God] finds collaboration of a kind which makes a decisive contribution to the completion of his creative work."[8] In the same vein François Russo observes that the scientist today is not driven so much to contemplate the truth (as if it were objective to him like a blueprint) as to achieve it. He explains further by designating "the secret intention of the scientist" as the urge to "reveal" the truth about matter. He quotes Ladriere approvingly, who describes science as the "process through which the world as nature finds its fulfillment and its apotheosis in the world as logos."[9]

A corollary of the awareness of the role of man and his creative freedom in the creation of the world is an openness regarding scientific methodology. The world does not disclose a single so-called scientific method. "The first observation to be made about the scientific method," says Harold

Schilling, "is . . . that there is no such thing—as it is ordinarily conceived."[10] Science thrives not with a formal logic or method, but rather in "creative, imaginative reasoning." To realize that the question of method is fluid and open is to realize only that the scientist is more significant for science than is the method he may for the moment employ.

John Dillenberger quite rightly warns against the efforts of theology to capitalize on this openness and indecision. We have seen that nature does not reveal God to man—either in its disclosures or its mystery, its determinism or indeterminism. Man, rather, discloses God to it; man's knowledge of the world is, in Ladriere's words, the "apotheosis" of nature. But despite Dillenberger's warning about using scientific models in theology, I am inclined to see in Heisenberg's discovery of indeterminacy the discovery that man affects, indeed creates, the world he knows. This is a problem for the positivist, for him who fails to understand the personal nature of scientific knowledge; but to us it should be clear that the principle of indeterminacy is a symbol of man, and a call to man to fill the void and the indeterminant not with God and supernatural notions, but with man and scientific discovery.

Notes

1. See Ramsey's *Models and Mystery* (London: Oxford University Press, 1964), p. 16.
2. See Ramsey's discussion of the metaphors of theology which rise from "some insight and inspiration" (*ibid.*, pp. 55 ff.). This is what I mean by an intuitive symbol.
3. Gordon Kaufman, who in my judgment rightly insists that the models of Christian theology are personal and historical, misses the full implication of his own method as he reflects on the nature of the created realm. His thinking becomes inexplicably static and rationalistic when he states, for instance, that the world is a "cosmos," that faith "believes there is an underlying structure sustained by the God of order" (note: not the God of history), that this structure is "characterized by logic, reason and order." He fails to see

that essential to nature as created by God is man himself in his personal history as scientist. See Kaufman, *Systematic Theology* (New York: Scribner's, 1968), pp. 37 ff. and p. 296.

4. Dillenberger. *Protestant Thought and Natural Science* (Garden City, N.Y.: Doubleday, 1960), p. 268.
5. See Harvey Cox's *The Secular City* (New York: Macmillan, 1965), pp. 21–24, where he shows that the Christian doctrine of creation takes God out of world and nature.
6. *Christians in a Technological Era*, ed. Hugh C. White (New York: Seabury Press, 1964), p. 28.
7. *Ibid.*, p. 40.
8. *Ibid.*, p. 93. Note that Morel tends toward a rationalism with his reference to "God's plan," suggesting perhaps some objective blueprint which would belittle the freedom and creativity of man (see p. 87).
9. *Ibid.*, pp. 96–97.
10. Schilling, *Science and Religion* (New York: Scribner's, 1962), p. 40.

The Doctrine of the Spirit and the Task of a Theology of Nature

Wolfhart Pannenberg

Making his second contribution to the *New Theology* series—his first was the essay "Appearance as the Arrival of the Future" in number 2 (1968)—German theologian Wolfhart Pannenberg in the present essay is concerned to redefine the concept of spirit "within the broad horizon of an overall interpretation of life." After criticizing the subjectivistic bias of traditional Christian piety and thought in dealing with the spirit, Dr. Pannenberg turns to the thought of Paul Tillich and Teilhard de Chardin, which he finds more helpful in this regard. He discusses the similarities and differences of their thought on spirit and life, and then amplifies and to some extent revises their views as groundwork for a proposal of his own: "using the self-transcendence of life as a clue to the phenomenon of the spirit and as a basis for a redefinition of spiritual reality." Professor of systematic theology at the University of Mainz, Dr. Pannenberg is the author of such works as *Theology and the Kingdom of God, Jesus: God and Man, What Is Man?*, and *Basic Questions in Theology* (2 vols.). His article—from the January 1972 issue of *Theology*,* a publication of the Anglican Church's Society for Promoting Christian Knowledge—was partly delivered as a lecture at King's College, London, on November 2, 1971, but had to go unfinished because of a bomb hoax.

I

WHEN THE SECOND ecumenical council at Constantinople in 381 complemented the Creed of Nicaea,

* S.P.C.K., Holy Trinity Church, Marylebone Rd., London, N.W., 1.

the first of the additions to its third article was to call the Holy Spirit the one who gives life (πνεῦμα ζωοποιοῦν). This language, of course, was no innovation, but was reminiscent of the way the New Testament writings had spoken of the Spirit. Especially Paul and John had called the Spirit the quickening one, the one who gives life. Today this is often interpreted in a restrictive way as a purely soteriological expression referring to the new life of faith, and certainly this is in the focus of the early Christian writings. But the phrase is by no means to be restricted to the life of faith. There are a number of words which in mentioning the life-giving spirit explicitly refer to the resurrection of the dead. And at least Paul alludes to the breath of life (πνοὴ ζωῆς) that according to Gen 2: 7 was given to the first man, when he says, I Cor. 15: 45, that while the first man was created a living soul, the last man will be life-giving spirit. That Adam was created a living soul is an explicit quotation from Gen. 2: 7. There it is presented as an effect of the breath of life being inspired by God into man's nose. This breath of life (πνοὴ ζωῆς) was taken by Philo of Alexandria as spirit of life (πνευμα ζωῆς), and in a similar way Paul's assertion that the second Adam will be life-giving spirit and not only a living soul refers to the breath of life which God inspired into the human body when he created man. Thus, if we want to understand Paul's idea of the new existence of man, we have first to explore the Old Testament background of his statement. It is precisely the idea of the spirit as the origin of all life.

This idea was very common in the ancient world. It was considered an empirical fact that with the last breath life is leaving the body. Hence the mysterious power of life was widely understood to be identical with breath. Therefore, the soul as the power of life, and breath and spirit were closely related, not only in the Ancient Near East, but also in Greek thought. πνεῦμα and πνοὴ or breath were associated, and by πνεῦμα nothing else was meant but the air that we breathe. This explains how one of the earliest Greek philosophers, Anaximenes from Milet, came to consider the air as the origin of all things. It was on this line that later on Anaxagoras proclaimed the mind as the ruler of the cosmos, the difference being mainly that Anaximenes had considered the human soul as example of the air that pervades everything, while Anaxagoras took it the other way round and conceived of the power pervading the cosmos by analogy with the highest ability of the human soul.

The relation between breath and air permits a closer understanding of the fact that in the Old Testament the divine spirit was closely associated with wind and storm. Thus in the very beginning of the creation, according to Genesis I, the spirit of God stirred up the waters of the primeval ocean. And the prophet Ezekiel in his great vision of his people's dry and dead bones on the plain saw the spirit of God breathing into the bones after they had taken on flesh and bringing them to life again.

The most pathetic description of the creative function of the divine spirit with regard to life has been given in Psalm 104. The psalm speaks to God of his creatures: "When thou hidest thy face, they are dismayed, when thou takest away their breath, they die and return to their dust. When thou sendest forth thy spirit, they are created; and thou renewest the face of the ground." The last phrase identifies the divine spirit with those prolific winds that renew the surface of the ground in springtime. Jahweh's spirit had taken over this function from Baal who was a God of storm as well as of fertility.

The life-giving activity of the divine spirit determines the horizon for all other functions which the Old Testament attributes to the spirit of God. There is especially the charismatic element. Not only for prophetic vision and inspiration, but also for the work of the artist, for poets and heroes, a special endowment with the spirit of God was considered necessary. These charismatic phenomena, however, were taken to refer to the same power that inspires and animates all life. The charismatic phenomena present just outstanding examples of life. They exhibit a particularly intensified life and are therefore attributed to an exceptional share in the life-giving spirit.

In a similar way Paul's idea of the new life of the resurrection is based on the traditional understanding of life as originating from the creative power of the spirit. The ordinary life is not life in the full sense of the word, because it is perishable. The living beings have only a limited share in the power of life, for according to Gen. 6: 3 God has decided that his spirit should not continue to be active in man indefinitely, for after all man is only flesh. Therefore the time of his life is limited. When he expires, "the dust returns to the earth as it was, and the spirit returns to God who gave it," says Ecclesiastes (9: 7). This, of course, does not imply any immortality of the human soul, but rather its dissolution into the divine spirit of whom it came. Paul discovered an indication for the limited character of the present life in the Genesis report itself, since it speaks only of a living being or soul springing from the creative breath of life. This meant to Paul that the living being is different from the spirit himself, and this fact accounts for the perishable character of our lives. Since our life in form of a soul or a living being is separated from its origin in the creative spirit of God, it has fallen to death. Therefore the question can arise for another life, a true life that persists in communication with its spiritual source. Precisely this comes to expression in Paul's idea of the resurrection life that will be one with the life-giving spirit and therefore immortal. Again, this was not a completely strange idea within the stream of Jewish tradition. Had not the prophets announced a time when the spirit of God will remain on his people and even be poured out on all flesh? The precise meaning of this is nothing less than immortal life, and therefore the resurrection of Christ and the spread of the proclamation of it could be taken as the beginning of the fulfilment of the old promises. In the New Testament the spirit is closely connected with the resurrected Lord, and the presence of the spirit in the Christian community should not be severed from the ongoing proclamation of the resurrection of Christ and from the participation in it by faith and hope. Thus although the emphasis of the New Testament writings concerning the spirit is on the new life of faith communicated by the spirit and on his charismatic presence, the deep meaning of those affirmations and their particular logic and rationality is only accessible if one takes into account the basic convictions of the Jewish tradition concerning the spirit as the creative origin of all life.

II

In Greek patristic theology, as in the Eastern Orthodox tradition until the present time, there has always been preserved a continuous awareness of the fundamental importance of the spirit's participation in the act of creation as providing the basis for the significance of his soteriological presence in the Church and in Christian experience. Certainly, a characteristic intellectualization took place, since the spirit was identified with the wisdom of God. Thus Irenaeus, in order to confirm his assertion that the spirit was already present and active in the creation of the world, appealed to Proverbs 3: 19: "The Lord by wisdom founded the earth, by understanding he established the heavens, by his spirit the deeps broke forth and the clouds drop down the dew." He also referred to the myth of Wisdom in Proverbs 8 and concluded that the one God has made and ordered everything through his word and his wisdom. But in spite of the intellectualistic overtones of the Wisdom tradition, Irenaeus related the spirit especially to the prophetic inspirational experiences, and regarded them as a specific example for the more general fact that the spirit of God "from the very beginning" assisted all men in adjusting themselves to the actions of God by announcing the future, reporting the past and interpreting the present. Thus the spirit, according to Irenaeus, was the first to reveal God to humanity. Afterwards the Son adopted us and only in the *eschaton* God will be known as Father in the kingdom of heaven.

Although since the third century the soteriological function of the spirit as a special divine assistance toward the ethical destiny of man attracted more and more attention, particularly with the rise of the monastic movement, Athanasius and after him Basil of Caesarea very strongly emphasized the collaboration of the spirit in the work of creation in order to assure his full divinity. In the Latin church this aspect was hardly ever treated with comparable seriousness. The activity of the Holy Spirit was seen in connection with charity and grace rather than with the creation of life, and the period of the Spirit in the history of salvation was no longer identified with the period of the preparation of mankind for the arrival of the Son of God, but rather with the period of the Church after the incarnation and after Pentecost. Thus it is not surprising that, with regard to the Reformers, Prenter and other authors have spoken of a rediscovery of the doctrine of the Spirit. Of course, the Spirit had never been altogether forgotten in Christian theology. But in mediaeval theology even in the doctrine of grace the Spirit receded into the background of the idea of a created grace that was considered the supernatural gift communicated through the sacraments. The Reformers, however, because of their biblicism rediscovered and reappropriated for their theology the broad application of the idea of the Spirit in the Biblical writings. In this connection, Luther as well as Calvin strongly emphasized the role of the Spirit in the creation, but neither of them developed in a systematic way the consequences for an understanding of nature. This fact explains in part why Protestant theology afterwards fell back to a predominantly soteriological conception of the work of the Spirit. This is particularly true of pietism. In the beginning of the 17th century Johann Arndt was silent concerning the contribution of the Spirit to the work of creation, Jean de Labadie explicitly denied it, and later on Philipp Jacob Spener mentioned it, but treated it like a piece of dead tradition. Thus the Spirit became a factor in subjective experience rather than a principle in explanation of nature. The Cartesian dualism of spirit and matter certainly contributed to the pervading and lasting influence of this subjective interpretation of the doctrine of the spirit.

The subjectivistic bias was further enhanced by the influence of the spiritualistic movement of the 16th and 17th centuries which developed from mediaeval mysticism. In this tradition, which also influenced pietism, the Spirit was related to anthropology although not to the world of nature. The Spirit was conceived in correspondence to the inner light in the human mind. This paved the way for the identification of spirit and mind in the idealist tradition under the impact of Cartesian dualism. Even John Locke conceived of the spirit in terms of a substance acting in the operations of the mind, and because David Hume eliminated the idea of substance, he could abolish the idea of spirit altogether. The idealist thinkers, on the other hand, and especially Hegel, developed a new perspective of the universe as created by the Spirit. But they did so on the basis of the Cartesian dualism and of the identification of spirit with mind. Precisely this point proved fatal for idealism, because spirit as absolute mind was shown to be an absolutizing self-projection of the human mind. Thus the identification of spirit and mind became an important argument for the atheism of Feuerbach and his famous followers. Christian theology, on the other hand, argued against idealism because of the identification of the divine spirit with the human spirit. This resulted in separating the spirit from the human mind. But then theological talk about the divine spirit lost its last empirical correlate, and consequently it has become almost meaningless. The only function left to it is that of a pretended legitimation for the acceptance of otherwise unintelligible statements of faith. Such an explanation of the work of the spirit is far from overcoming the subjectivism that has been so characteristic of Christian piety in modern times. On the contrary, it represents the peak of that subjectivism, a subjectivism of an irrational decision of faith.

It should be obvious that the appeal to a principle beyond understanding in order to render acceptable what otherwise remains unintelligible does not provide an adequate basis for a responsible doctrine of the Holy Spirit in theology. Nor can we build such a doctrine on the identification of spirit with mind after that has come under so serious and pertinent criticism in the history of modern thought. Nor is it advisable to start again with the reality allegedly disclosed in religious experience, particularly in the experience of "spiritual" regeneration, for that would end up again in the deadlock of subjectivism. In order to find a fresh starting point in the tradition, we have to go back behind the entire subjectivistic thrust in the history of the doctrine, even behind the isolation of the soteriological concern in dealing with the spirit. Only an understanding of the spirit on the basis of his function in creation and this regard to his contribution to an explanation of nature can overcome the subjectivistic bias of traditional Christian piety and thought in dealing with the spirit. But can we in any intellectually serious way attribute a function in the explanation of nature to the Holy Spirit?

III

In modern Christian thought there are two outstanding examples of an attempt to break through the spiritual subjectivism and to develop a conception of the spirit within the broad horizon of an overall interpretation of life. One is the section on life and the spirit in Paul Tillich's *Systematic Theology*. The other one is the vision developed by Teilhard de Chardin of the evolutionary process of life as being directed by a spiritual power.

For Tillich, spirit is one of the "dimensions of life" beside the inorganic, the organic and the psychological dimension. They are potentially present in every living being. Among them spirit is the "power of animation" and therefore distinct from the different parts of the organic system. Spirit is not identical with mind, although on the level of human life the self-awareness of the animal is taken up into the personal-communal dimension which Tillich calls spirit. Thus man is that organism in which the dimension of spirit has become dominant. On the other hand, even the human spirit cannot overcome the ambiguities of life in its constitutive functions of self-integration, self-creation and self-transcendence. In order to cope with these ambiguities, the divine spirit must assist the human spirit. Tillich thus distinguishes between divine and human spirit. Only by ecstatic acts the human spirit participates in the divine spirit, and only in this way he can approach the integration and unity of the three regions of spiritual life, culture, morality and religion.

Tillich himself observed a close similarity of his perspective to Teilhard de Chardin, whose book about "the phenomenon of man" he read after the completion of his own work. There exists indeed a basic similarity in the idea that spirit is the animating power of all life and not identical with mind, although in the emergence of the human consciousness it realizes itself in a decisively new and intensified form. Teilhard and Tillich also agree in emphasizing the tendency of self-transcendence in life, that was called radial energy by Teihard while in Tillich's view it relates the human spirit to the divine spirit.

There are also differences, however, between the two approaches. First, Teilhard does not distinguish in the same way as Tillich does between the divine spirit and spirit as a dimension of life. In Teilhard's perspective there is only one spirit permeating and activating all the material processes and urging them beyond themselves in a process of progressive spiritualization and of converging unification towards a center of perfect unity that in providing the end of the evolutionary process proves to be its true dynamic origin. In such a perspective, created spirit can be only a participation in the dynamics of the one spirit that animates the entire process of evolution. The difference between God and man is preserved also in such a perspective, because only in transcending itself a material being participates in the spiritual dynamic. This corresponds to Tillich's emphasis on the self-transcendence of life and on the element of ecstasy in spiritual experience. Tillich presumably retained the dualism of spirit and divine Spirit because of his method of correlation between question and answer. In reality, however, even within his conception it is difficult to see why the ecstatic element is attributed specifically to the "spiritual presence" of God in faith, hope, and love, and not universally to all spiritual experience as exemplifying the self-transcendence of life.

A second difference is that Teilhard does not use the vague and confusing language of "dimensions of life"—a language which at best has metaphorical value in exposing the "one dimensional" narrow-mindedness of a purely materialistic description of organic life. The weakness of such metaphorical talk about "dimensions of life" consists in the fact that there is, of course, no coordinate system of the dimensions of inorganic, psychological and spiritual reality. The same interest in the depth of the phenomenon of life that escapes a purely materialistic description is expressed by Teilhard in a much simpler way, when Teilhard spoke of a spiritual inside of every material phenomenon. He shared this view with the old tradition of philosophical animism. But he also offered a justification for it, first by appealing to the principle that scientific exploration should look for the universal rule behind an apparently extraordinary phenomenon as the emergence of the human mind is, and second by maintaining a regular correspondence between the degree of complexity of a physical phenomenon and the level of its interior spirituality. Teilhard's boldest assertion, however, consists in his combination of the spiritual inside of natural phenomena with the energy behind the natural processes.

In the final analysis, Teilhard supposed, all energy is spiritual in character. But since energy manifests itself for physical observation in the interrelations of physical phenomena, Teilhard introduced his famous distinction between a tangential energy or force that accounts for all sorts of "solidarity" of the bodily elements and their interrelations, and a radial energy, that explains the self-transcendence of existing phenomena towards increasing complexity and unity. This distinction is due, as I mentioned before, to the basic assertion of the spiritual character of energy. The natural scientists, especially the physicists, concern themselves—as Teilhard explicitly affirmed—only with the exterior manifestation of the cosmic energy in the interrelations of bodies. But if energy, as Teilhard assumes, is essentially spiritual, then there must be another aspect of energy, and this is to be found in the dynamics of self-transcendence which Teilhard calls radial energy.

The problems inherent in this idea become particularly apparent if one asks for aspects of the concept of energy that have not been taken into consideration in Teilhard's thought. Here, the phenomenon of an energetic field deserves particular attention. Classical mechanics dealt with bodies, with their positions in space and time and with the forces effective in their interrelations. These forces were attributed to the bodies that were understood to exercise a force. But when physical science attempted to reduce the notion of a natural force to a property of the body, especially to its mass, that did not work. For the last time Einstein started on such an attempt. But his theory of relativity ended up with the contrary result. Instead of reducing space to a property of bodies and of their interrelations, it in fact resulted in a conception of matter as a function of space. This marks the definitive turning point from a conception of natural force on the basis of the model of the moving body to an autonomous idea of energy conceived of as a field. The attribution of natural forces to a field of energy, as, e.g., in the case of an electric or magnetic field, means to conceive of energy as the primary reality that transcends the body through which it may manifest itself —a reality that we no longer need to attribute to a body as its subject.

Teilhard de Chardin did not yet fully appreciate this radical change of the concept of natural force from a property of bodies to an independent reality that only manifests itself in the genesis and movements of bodies. To be sure, Teilhard recognized the idea of energy as the most fundamental idea of physics. But he expressed reservations concerning Einstein's field theory. He insisted on the connection of energy to the body, and he expressed this connection by conceiving of energy as a sort of soul even in inorganic bodies.

In treating Teilhard's idea of spirit, the lengthy discussion of the problems connected with the concept of energy may have seemed at first a deviation. Now it becomes apparent that Teilhard's decision for not conceiving energy in terms of a field, but in terms of the inside reality of bodies, has had far-reaching consequences for his understanding of the spirit. In fact, in a certain way it counteracted his basic emphasis on the spirit as a transcendent principle, transcending every given reality but activating it in the direction of a creative unification. If Teilhard had conceived of energy in terms of a field, this would have been in perfect concordance with his idea of a transcendent spirit whose creative power dominates the entire process of evolution. Since, however, he identified energy as the inside reality of bodies, he attributed energy to those bodies. Therefore, even the movement of self-transcendence and thus the entire dynamic of evolution was attributed to finite bodies rather than—as Teilhard wanted to do—to a principle transcending them as is the case with his point Omega. Thus the basic ambiguity of Teilhard's thought comes to the fore, the ambiguity of what finally sets in motion the evolutionary process: point Omega or the evolving entities themselves. On the basis that energy is attributed to the bodies, the process and the direction of evolution seems to be produced by the evolving species which seem to act like subjects of their own evolution. In this perspective point Omega appears to be a mere extrapolation of tendencies inherent in the evolutionary process or, more precisely, in the evolving animals themselves. But on the other hand, Teilhard wants to explain Omega, the goal of the process of evolution, as being its true creative origin. This he did by describing evolution as the work of a unified spirit who transcends the individual entities and is finally identical with God Omega who creatively and progressively unifies his world.

But Teilhard failed to relate this view adequately to his idea of energy, although spirit and energy designate the same reality in his thought. He conceived of energy only as inside of bodies instead of a field transcending the bodies and prior to them. If he had done so, Teilhard could have developed his basic intuition of the world as a process of creative unification by a spiritual dynamic in a more consistent and more convincing way. He need not even surrender the concept of a spiritual inside of bodily phenomena. He had only to add that this is the aspect of the universal field of energy from the finite point of view of the entities through which it manifests itself. They participate in the universal field of energy only by transcending themselves, or by way of ecstasy, and the degree of their capability for that ecstatic experience would mark the degree of their spirituality. Thus, Paul Tillich's idea of the ecstatic character of spiritual presence gets an application far beyond the specific spirituality of the Christian faith, love, and hope, which it was designed for. Instead of pointing to a peculiarity of Christian experience, it turns out representing a basic element of reality and particularly of organic life.

IV

The proposed revision of Teilhard's conception of evolution meets a number of the most serious arguments against his thought. Especially it permits one to abandon the idea of a teleological guidance of the evolutionary process and to give much more importance to the element of chance or contingency in shaping that process. But is it really justifiable to use the term spirit in order to designate the energy working in the evolutionary process? And has such a description any theological significance? Is there any substantial continuity with the way in which the Christian tradition referred to the Spirit of God as the creative origin of all life?

I shall discuss this question by asking first for the conditions for an adequate translation of the biblical idea of a creative spirit as origin of all life into the context of modern thought. Such an explanation will provide certain criteria, and these criteria can be applied afterwards to Teilhard's ideas and to the model that emerged from our discussion of them.

Every attempt for a translation of ideas has first to consider the gulf that should be bridged over. Most of the differences between the biblical and the modern understanding of life can be derived from the fact that the biblical idea of life works with the assumption of an origin of life that transcends the living being, as it was empirically evident to the ancient world in the phenomenon of breath, while the modern biological science conceives of life as function of the living cell that reproduces itself. At a first glance, this comparison gives the impression of a strict opposition between the modern immanentistic view of life and the explanation of life by a transcendent principle as it was offered by the Old Testament. Compared with this basic opposition, the identification of that transcendent principle as spirit appears to be of secondary importance. A closer look, however, reveals that there is more than that apparent opposition. On the one hand, the biblical perspective is quite open for the idea of independent existence which constitutes the very essence of the concept of a living being: it has life in itself. On the other hand, modern biology does not exclude everything that transcends the living cell from the analysis of life. Although life is taken as the activity of the living cell or of a higher organism, that activity itself is conditioned. It is conditioned particularly by the requirement of an appropriate environment. When kept in isolation, no organism is fit for life. In this sense, every organism depends on specific conditions for its life, and these conditions do not remain extrinsic to its own reality, but contribute to the character of its life: an organism lives "in" its environment. It not only needs and actively occupies a territory, but it turns it into a means for his self-realization, it nourishes itself on its environment. In this sense, every organism lives beyond itself. Again it becomes evident that life is essentially ecstatic: it takes place in the environment of the organism much more than in itself.

But is there any relation of this ecological self-transcendence of life to the biblical idea of a spiritual origin of life? I think there is. In order to recognize this correspondence we must first focus what has been said about the phenomenal character of spirit and keep in suspense for the time being the divine nature of the spirit. Then it becomes evident that breath belongs to the most important environmental conditions of life. Only if there is fresh air can the organic processes go on. Hence breath can be taken as an appropriate illustration of the dependence of the organism on its environment. To be sure, breath can no longer be regarded the proper cause of life. At this point, every modern account of life has to confess its difference from the primitive explanation of life that was equalled also in the biblical writings. There is, however, an element of truth in that primitive explanation, and the first clue to it is to be found in the dependence of the organism on its environment.

It would be hardly defensible of course to maintain that an organism is created by its environment, although an appropriate environment is a necessary condition for its existence. But there is still another aspect of its living beyond itself: by turning its environment into the place and means of its life, the organism relates itself at the same time to its own future and, more precisely, to a future of its own transformation. This is true of every act of self-creation and nourishing and developing itself, by regenerating and reproducing its life. By his drives an animal is related to although not necessarily aware of his individual future and to the future of his species. This also belongs to the ecstatic character of the self-transcendence of life, and this is what Teilhard de Chardin called radial energy. It comes to most emphatical expression in the increasing complexity and final convergence of the evolutionary process of life, but it is present even in the life of the individual and specifically in the temporal aspect of his self-transcendence. Now, if it was correct to revise Teilhard's account of radial energy in terms of a field of energy that shapes a process of evolution, then it makes sense also to maintain that this field of energy manifests itself in the self-transcendence of the living being, and thereby it even creates the lives of the individuals. Hence, the element of truth in the old image of breath as being the creative origin of life is not exhausted by the dependence of the organism on its environment, but contains a deeper mystery closely connected with the ecological self-transcendence of life: the temporal self-transcendence of every living being is a specific phenomenon of organic life that separates it from inorganic structures.

At this point, there arise a number of questions that would deserve further investigation. In the first place, there is a question concerning the relation between ecology and genetics. The argument for the self-transcendence of life has been developed largely on the basis of ecological evidence. Does it also apply to genetics? If this were not so, the assumption of a field of energy effective in the self-transcendence of life would loose much of its persuasion. A second question concerns the character of that field itself: is it legitimate to use the concept of a field when the impact of the future on the present is at stake, as it is the case with Teilhard's point Omega and with his assertion of a creative influence of Omega on the entire evolutionary process? Applied in such a way, the concept of a field replaces the age-old teleological language. Does it really fit the purpose? In any case, the temporal structure of field theories needs to be further investigated, especially in the light of the problems of the quantum theory that no longer abstracts from the question of time as other field theories do. This also involves the element of contingency in the effectiveness of such a field. Finally, granted the possibility of speaking about the creative effectiveness of Teilhard's point Omega in terms of a field of energy, its relevance for the phenomenon of spirit is still to be explained.

V

The discussion of Tillich's and Teilhard's views on spirit and life resulted in the proposal of using the self-transcendence of life as a clue to the phenomenon of the spirit and as a basis for a redefinition of spiritual reality. This proposal owes part of its inspiration to Tillich's idea of the ecstatic character of "spiritual presence," but it does not follow his separation of that ecstatic experience from the process of life that is ultimately nourished on self-transcendence. Tillich accepted a separation of his idea of spiritual presence from the continuously self-transcending process of life, because he conceived of self-transcendence only in terms of an activity of the organism. But after the discussion of Teilhard's ideas of spirit and energy and particularly after having replaced Teilhard's "radial energy" by the assumption of a field of energy effective in the evolutionary process, we can conceive of self-transcendence in a more complex way: self-transcendence is to be regarded at the same time as an activity of the organism and as an effect of a power that continuously raises the organism beyond its limitations and thereby grants it its life. The functions of the self-creation and self-integration of life depend on the ongoing process of its self-transcendence. If the self-transcendent tendency of life could be exhaustively explained in terms of an autonomous activity of the organism, there would be no room left for the assumption of a spiritual reality involved in his life.

The term spirit in its broad application to the total sphere of life refers to the fact that the self-transcending activity of organic life is to be explained within a broader context as it is provided by the process of evolution towards a definitive self-assertion of life, but also by its abundant production of fragmentary symbols of the power and beauty of life, the results of its self-creative and self-integrative activity that anticipates the final goal of the evolutionary process.

The redefinition of the concept of spirit on the basis of the self-transcending tendency in all organic life unties the association of spirit with mind. Spirit is not identical with mind, nor is it manifested primarily through mind. Rather, the reflective nature of the human mind represents a particular form and degree of participation in the spiritual power, and that is closely connected with the particular mode of human self-transcendence.

Man does not only live beyond himself in his environment and on its supplies. He does not in fact only change his environment by claiming it as his. But he is able deliberately to change his world in order to change the conditions for his own existence. That presupposes first that man is able to consider the realities of his world on their own terms, not only in relation to his drives. He can be "with" the things different from himself in a way no other animal is. The second presupposition of the deliberate transformation of the world by human activity is that man is able to project a future in distinction from his present. That makes him master of the present. Both these aspects imply that man can take a stand beyond himself and look at himself from a distance. In other words, he has the capacity for reflexion. The continuously reflective consciousness of man emphatically illustrates his particular mode of being beyond himself. And precisely in being beyond himself he is himself, not only this individual, but a human being. In taking a stand beyond himself, the human mind is no longer himself the unity of his experience, but is looking for something beyond himself that gives unity to his experiences. We apprehend the particular only within a wider horizon of meaning which is anticipated as some sort of unity. This underlies all processes of abstractive thinking. But the unity beyond the individual is also concrete in form of a community of individuals. Hence in the reflective consciousness of man the importance of social life for the individual develops to a new level: the social community in its difference from individual existence becomes constitutive for the individual's experience of the unity and identity of his existence. In this particular way man is a social being, not simply as a member of the flock, but by recognizing the community as manifesting a unity of human nature superior to his individuality. Since, however, the society is composed of individuals, the final basis of its unity is to be asked for beyond the concrete institutions of social life: as social being man is at the same time the religious being.

It is obvious that the particular mode of human self-transcendence characterizes all the specifically spiritual activities and achievements of man. It comes to expression in the human ability for conceiving abstract ideas as well as in trust, love, and hope. It is basic for the quest of the individual for personal identity as well as for his social life and its institutions, and last not least for his creation of a world of meaning by developing language and by creating a world of culture. In all this, man is at the same time creative and receptive of the spiritual reality that raises him beyond himself. The most creative acts of his spiritual activity provide the most impressive evidence for this assertion: the creative design of an artist, the sudden discovery of a truth, the experience of being liberated for a moment of significant existence, the power of a moral commitment—all this comes to us by a sort of inspiration. All these experiences testify to a power that raises our hearts, the power of the spirit. When man is most creative, he most self-consciously participates in the spiritual power beyond himself. But its presence does not only characterize the exceptional moments of elevation, but also permeates the general structure of human behaviour in its openness beyond himself. The exceptional experiences of spiritual freedom and creativity illuminate the general condition of human existence.

And yet, human life is not yet fully united to the spirit. There are the hours when we live in low spirits or even let ourselves be taken in by a bad spirit. There are the occasions when we sadly realize the absence of true unity and meaning from our lives. There are the conflicts, repression and violence among individuals and in the relations between the individual and his social world. There is failure and guilt, disability, disease and death. There are flashes of meaning, but only in a fragmentary way, and the wholeness of life remains an open question at the moment of death. There is, indeed, ample space for the ambiguities of human life, the dialectic which Paul Tillich so eloquently described. In face of all this, the presence of loving concern, of mutual trust, of meaning and hope is almost a supernatural event, especially if it constitutes a continuous identity and integrity of our lives in spite of all its precariousness. And in this way the Christian proclamation, with its assurance of a new life that will be no more subject to death, communicates a new and undisturbed confidence, a new and continuous spiritual presence. Its very heart lies in the confidence of being united to the future of God, a confidence that became incarnate in the existence of Christ and is effective in human history from that time on. The spirit, however, of this new spiritual presence that is a life in the community of faith, is no other spirit than the spirit that animates and quickens all life. And only because it is the same spirit that created all life by inspiring its abundant self-transcendence, it provides no escapist opiate, but the power of enduring under and finally overcoming the absurdities and adversities of the present world.

The Ethics of Nature and Nurture

Van Rensselaer Potter

Deeply concerned by what he sees as an identity crisis of unprecedented dimensions within the scientific community—a crisis precipitated by the separation of value judgments from the arena of the scientific enterprise—Van Rensselaer Potter has been concerned to develop a new discipline called *bioethics*, which would combine human value considerations with science in general and especially with the "realities" of biological science in the Man/Earth relationship. Dr. Potter, professor of oncology at the University of Wisconsin Medical School, introduced his concept of bioethics in his book *Bioethics: Bridge to the Future*. Here he further expands that concept, particularly in the context of his opposition to what he calls "cultural laissez-faire." His article, from the March 1973 issue of *Zygon*,* is a slightly altered version of a paper he presented at the Star Island Conference on Technology and the Human Future, held on Star Island near Portsmouth, N. H., in the summer of 1972.

Introduction

In 1962 I was invited to participate in a celebration of the one hundredth anniversary of the Morrill Act, which established the land-grant colleges. I chose as my theme "The Concept of Human Progress" and spent most of my allotted time arguing two main points: first, that progress is not inevitable and second, that widely held concepts of human progress would have to be drastically revised if humanity is to survive. This essay was my first step in a

* 5700 Woodlawn Ave., Chicago, Ill. 60637.

series that finally led to the publication of a small volume in which the new hope for a "bridge to the future" crystallized in a word—*bioethics.*[1] In my innocence, it never occurred to me that the concept of "progress" was inherently fictional, if not actually sinful, in the minds of many scholars who had devoted a great deal of thought to the subject. I never doubted the validity of the concept as a goal. It was just that I assumed that there were several kinds of progress and that all of them came at a price. My acquaintance with the concept grew out of my training as a biologist and also from a fortuitous purchase in 1958 of a secondhand copy of Darwin's *Origin of Species* (6th edition) at Blackwell's. In his conclusion, Darwin commented that since "no cataclysm has desolated the whole world . . . we may look with some confidence to a secure future of great length." "And," he continued, "as natural selection works solely by and for the good of each being [surely an exaggeration], all corporeal and mental endowments will tend to progress towards perfection." As Darwin contemplated the future, he saw a world in which "A grand and almost untrodden field of inquiry will be opened, on the causes and laws of variation, on correlation, on the effects of use and disuse, on the direct action of external conditions, and so forth." In this one sentence we can see the germ of the whole subject of *Nature* and *Nurture*, the two forces that must be reckoned with if humanity is to survive and progress. Darwin never doubted either survival or progress for mankind. Today we are sure of neither, and thoughtful individuals everywhere are earnestly convening in search of answers. With the interjection of the issue of survival, the old question takes on a new urgency. We no longer can ask merely which *is* more important, nature or nurture? Today, we are impelled to inquire what *ought* we to do, or what *must* we do to survive? Thus the question becomes an ethical one, and we are confronted with an old question in a new frame: the moral decisions of ethics seen in the light of the facts of nature and nurture, which is what I believe bioethics is all about.

Subsequent to these first steps into Darwin's final pages, it became apparent that the concept of progress has a history with almost no beginning and no end. In a recent overview on "The Nature of the Darwinian Revolution," a leading student of Darwinism, Professor Ernst Mayr, emphasized that it was the *refutation* of the concept of an automatic upward evolution that Darwin had to accomplish, along with the refutation of at least five other widely held basic beliefs, in order to achieve fully what we now think of as the Darwinian Revolution.[2] Thus, despite the sentence I quoted from Darwin's final pages, Ernst Mayr emphasized that "Darwin's conclusion, to some extent anticipated by Lamarck, was that evolutionary change through adaptation and specialization by no means necessitated continuous betterment," in contrast to "every evolutionist before Darwin" who "had taken it for granted that there was a steady progress of perfection in the living world." According to Mayr, "This belief was a straightline continuation of the (static) concept of a scale of perfection, which was maintained even by the progressionists for whom each new creation represented a further advance in the plan of the Creator." Mayr goes on to note that the concept of progress to perfection has as its chief latter-day proponent Teilhard de Chardin, who thus derives his impetus from pre-Darwinian thought, while warmly supporting Darwinism as a symbol.

Although the Darwinian revolution is a movement that actually began about 250 years ago and is much more complex than the simple models of scientific revolutions proposed by T. S. Kuhn,[3] according to Mayr,[4] the history of the idea of "progress of perfection" is much older. John Passmore, a philosophy professor at the Australian National University, has just published a book for which the title *The Perfectibility of Man* was inspired by a quote from D. H. Lawrence: "The Perfectibility of Man! Ah, heaven, what a dreary theme!" Passmore's scope includes "Progress by Natural Development from Darwin to Teilhard" (chapter

12), but it is much broader. In his own words, "My theme is a vast one, and I have traced it through three thousand years of man's intellectual history, from Homer to the present day."[5]

Passmore's project covers virtually every ancient source that might have a bearing on the subject of Nature and Nurture, but as in the older instances it appears that he has posed the question "Is man perfectible?" outside of the issue regarding the survival of mankind, with the result that he does not explicitly ask, "Ought we to attempt the perfection of man?" It must be understood that by the "perfection of man" Passmore is really concerned throughout the book with the lesser goal of "improvement of the human condition" and particularly with the philosophic history of the idea.

In his section on "Perfecting by Social Action," Passmore comes closest to the Nature and Nurture problem. He opens the section as follows:

> Pelagius and Augustine agreed on one point—the alternatives were clear, at least at the extremes. Either man could perfect himself, by the exercise of his own free will, or else he could be perfected only by the infusion of God's grace. These were the poles between which Christian controversy fluctuated. In the seventeenth century, however, a third possibility began to be canvassed, cutting across the ancient quarrel between Pelagians and Augustinians. Perhaps men would be perfected not by God, not by the exercise of their own free will, not even by some combination of the two, but by the deliberate intervention of their fellow-men.[6]

—in other words, by what is meant by the word *nurture*, in the present context.

He sums up this section in the following words:

> *Beginning with the Renaissance, but with increasing confidence in the seventeenth century, men began to maintain that in their relationships to their fellow-men rather than in*

their relationships to God, lay their hope of perfection. "Perfection" was defined in moral rather than in metaphysical terms, and came gradually to be further particularized as "doing the maximum of good." It was no longer supposed that in order to act morally men must abjure self-love; self-love was harnessed to the improvement of the human condition. "Perfectibility" meant the capacity to be improved to an unlimited degree, rather than the capacity to reach, and rest in, some such ultimate end as "the vision of God" or "union with the One." If men are to be able to perfect one another without divine assistance, however, it has to be presumed that they are not invincibly corrupt. Hence perfectibilists, following in Locke's footsteps, rejected original sin. Indeed, they agreed with Locke that men have no inborn moral tendencies, no innate tendency to act well or to act badly, but only a tendency to pursue pleasure and avoid pain. [We will question this simplistic view later.]

This new "moral psychology" opened the way to the suggestion that men could be to an infinite degree improved by the use of appropriate social mechanisms—in the first place, education. Education, Locke suggested, consists in forming moral habits in children by associating certain of their activities with pleasure, especially pleasure in the form of commendation, and others with pain, especially in the form of blame. Hartley developed Locke's innovations into a systematic perfectibilism by working out in detail an associationist psychology, according to which men could be not only educated but reeducated to any desired pattern.

In the twentieth century, "behavioural" psychologies have taken the place of associatism, but the fundamental assumptions remain. Innate differences are unimportant; men can be moulded to any desired shape by employing the appropriate psychological procedures. The road to infinite improvement lies open, on this view, to man: the only question is whether he is prepared to seize the opportunities which psychological science now offers him.[7] [Italics added]

Here, certainly, is the epitome of the emphasis on *nurture* in improving the human condition and a glimpse of the background that seems to have led to the views of B. F. Skinner in our time.

Passmore also reviews the genetic approach to perfectibility, using H. J. Muller as the protagonist and P. B. Medawar,[8] with whom he agrees, as the antagonist. Thus, Medawar notes: "There seems to be no doubt that some large part of human fitness is vested in a mechanism which provides for a high degree of genetic inequality and inborn diversity, which makes sure that there are plenty of different kinds of human beings." Again: "This fact sets a limit to any purely theoretical fancies we may come to indulge in about the perfectibility of men."

Passmore concludes:

> To achieve perfection in any of its classical senses, as so many perfectibilists have admitted, it would first be necessary to cease to be human, to become godlike, to rise above the human condition. But a god knows nothing of love, or science, or art, or craft, of family and friends, of discovery, of pride in work. And can he really count as perfection a condition which excludes all of these, for the sake of eternity, of order, or of unalloyed enjoyment?
>
> In spite of these reflections, which might lead us to reject perfectibilism in any of its forms, it is very hard to shake off the feeling that man is capable of becoming something much superior to what he now is. This feeling, if it is interpreted in the manner of the more commonsensical Enlighteners, is not in itself irrational. There is certainly no *guarantee* that men will ever be any better than they now are; their future is not, as it were, underwritten by Nature. Nor is there any device, whether skillful government, or education, which is certain to ensure the improvement of man's condition. To that extent the hopes of the developmentalists or the governmentalists or the educators must certainly be abandoned. There is not the slightest ground for believing, either, with the anarchist, that if only the State could be destroyed and men could start fresh, all would be well. But we know from our own experience, as teachers or parents, that individual human beings can come to

be better than they once were, given care, and that wholly to despair of a child or a pupil is to abdicate what is one's proper responsibility. We know, too, that in the past men have made advances, in science, in art, in affection. Men, almost certainly, are capable of more than they have ever so far achieved. But what they achieve, or so I have suggested, will be a consequence of their remaining anxious, passionate, discontented human beings. To attempt, in the quest for perfection, to raise men above that level is to court disaster; there is no level above it, there is only a level below it. "To be man," Sartre has written, "means to reach towards being God." That is why he also described man as "useless passion." For certainly man is a "useless passion" if his passion is to be God. But his passions are not useless, if they help him to become a little more humane, a little more civilized.[9]

But today, in 1972, it is not enough to ask how to become "a little more humane, a little more civilized." To ask merely these questions is to assume that mankind will survive and remain at least as human and civilized as at present without any organized effort on the part of concerned and future-oriented individuals. It is against a background that questions this assumption that we must discuss the problem of nature and nurture. Survival can no longer be assumed.

The Morality of Intervention

In the discussion of the ethics of nature and nurture in relation to technology, there is a recurring issue that may as well be faced at the outset and set up as a basis for further discussion. The ethical problem is that of deciding when to intervene in the life of another person and when not to do so. In a simplified form, it is a key issue in medical ethics as exemplified in the Latin phrase *Primum non nocere*—"First, to do no harm"—a guideline that frequently leads to inaction. It was originally based upon the fact that most "patients" admittedly get well by themselves.

The admonition has less impact in the case of the patient who will certainly not recover by himself and for whom no quick and certain therapy is available. This instance is exemplified by the advanced cancer patient, for whom therapy is definitely on an experimental basis and at the level of brinkmanship with every move a calculated risk. I wish to use this example as a paradigm for the less clear examples that range through a spectrum of situations in the medical field to the paramedical areas and finally to the events that touch the lives of all of us either as *intervenor* or *intervenee*, as in the case of parents and offspring, teachers and students, or husbands and wives, noting that the roles can be played in either direction in various instances.

The issue of intervention goes far beyond the matter of avoiding harm to the patient, or intervenee, in general terms. It involves the propriety of one individual or of society "managing" or intervening in the life of another individual or group of individuals, even with the best of intentions and even when requested to do so by the individuals or by society. The problem is to find the line that divides professional service or friendship or love in any of its forms from the many custodial relationships that destroy human dignity. This question may seem paradoxical because as individuals we are being manipulated by other individuals and by society using all kinds of technology from the moment of our birth until the moment of our death. Even after death, the disposal of our body may not occur according to our wishes. What is more, we desperately need to be shaped and socialized by parents, schools, and society to avoid becoming mental basket cases. A newborn baby is totally incapable of becoming a human being without the intervention of other human beings. Even if it were to be provided with food, hygiene, and shelter, a newborn infant would not *become* a "human" being if the sustenance were provided mechanically. The very thought is revolting, but it would be technologically possible. Because it is technologically possible at the other end of the life-span, it is frequently carried out with the dying patient who could not possibly survive without mechanical aids in place of more personal support, but who cannot *remain* a "human" being with them.

In the case of the dying patient, medical technology, when authorized, cannot easily be withheld. Physicians and relatives are caught in an ethical dilemma in which they frequently expend vast sums of money to prolong a life by all possible means even when all personal contact has been lost, merely because of a conspiracy of silence in which people refuse to make decisions that they have not been prepared for. Society is going to have to develop guidelines for the ethics of intervention not only in the case of the dying patient but also in a number of other stages of life. It would seem to me that an ethical approach would be to regard the use of technology under circumstances that are totally dehumanizing as appropriate only when two conditions are met: (1) the situation is assumed to have a good chance of being only temporary and (2) the individual has a good chance of living out a substantial fraction of his life-span as an individual after recovery. Since neither of these conditions is met in the case of the dying patient the development of further guidelines is advocated.

It is strange that medical technology may be overemployed for many dying patients at the end of a long life-span (provided their relatives can afford it), but underemployed in the case of the patient in the prime of life who cannot afford the technology that could prolong his life. In this category, the patient with failing kidneys is a classic example, although others could be cited.

If the patient can be helped by technology to live and function in terms that are acceptable to him, society should help him bear the burden; but whenever he is convinced that his human functions cannot be maintained, he should be given every possible assistance and moral support that will permit him to die with dignity and not be saddled with the impression that suicide is inherently sinful. This line of thought can be applied to a number of other human situations.

The ethics of nature and nurture from the medical standpoint is perhaps most poignant in the case of the mental patient vis-à-vis the role of psychiatrists, relatives, and friends. There seems to be considerable confusion as to what extent a psychotic or mildly neurotic patient should be managed and to what extent he should be left to his own resources. With the advent of the new drugs, the situation has become complicated by the aggressive advertising of some sectors of the pharmaceutical industry, in which physicians have been urged to prescribe tranquilizers for patients who are bothered by what some would consider the ordinary problems of daily living—for example, the woman who cannot communicate with her daughter-in-law or the co-ed newly arrived at a big university. The situation has degenerated to the point that editorial comment citing the above examples recently appeared in the prestigious *New England Medical Journal*.[10]

Psychiatrists, in general, have attempted to avoid telling a patient that it is his duty to do this or that, i.e., that he ought or ought not to do so and so. They have taken a strictly neutral position on what would seem to be valid ethical issues. Only a small minority of psychiatrists have taken the position that many patients might be desperately calling for advice and guidance rather than for just a technological fix in a capsule that would make them less sensitive to their environment. The alternative to the chemical fix is nearly always an attitude of cultural relativism, which decrees that the patient must choose his own standards of conduct and his own value system. However, the chemical fix should not be rejected out of hand. There must be many valid instances in which the proper combination of chemical fix and appropriate counseling will actually increase the ability of an individual to be a human being. But someone will have to decide for him. Instead of questioning some value systems and exalting others arrived at by an ongoing multidisciplinary dialog to help make such decisions, we find a conspiracy of silence, in which religion and science have forced psychiatrists, teachers, and parents into a cultural laissez-faire that casts youth, students, and troubled adults adrift in the turbulent stream of life.

The Role of Culture

Cultural laissez-faire can be deplored at the same time that cultural pluralism is advocated. The two concepts are not synonymous or analogous. Clifford Geertz has emphasized the role of culture in his article entitled "The Impact of the Concept of Culture on the Concept of Man."[11] He has proposed two very important ideas that must be emphasized and upheld if we are to argue against cultural laissez-faire on the one hand and uphold cultural pluralism on the other. Geertz proclaimed as broad generalizations the ideas that (1) culture is best seen not merely as complexes of concrete behavior patterns (customs, usages, traditions, habit clusters as described ad infinitum in *The Golden Bough*), but as a set of control mechanisms (plans, recipes, rules, instructions, or "programs" in the language of computer engineering) for the governing of human behavior and (2) man is precisely the animal most desperately dependent upon such extragenetic, outside-the-skin control mechanisms, such cultural programs, for ordering his behavior. Geertz emphasizes the view that culture is not something added on to a finished or virtually finished animal in the evolutionary sense, but that the slow, steady, almost glacial growth of culture over a million years altered the balance of selection pressures for evolving man in such a way as to play a major directive role in his evolution. The increasing reliance upon systems of significant symbols (language, art, myth, ritual) for orientation, communication, and self-control all created for man a new environment to which he was then obliged to adapt. Thus, in examining nature and nurture, we find that man's nature was evolving according to the pressures of his nurture, which included all of the components of his culture. Today we must ask what *ought* our culture do to increase the human use of human beings so that they will begin to approach the realization of their individual potentialities. But at the same time we must ask what *ought* society do to develop such a culture and what *ought* some of us do as individuals to help society develop such a culture. So we are back to Passmore's theme—the perfectibility of man, which we agree is limited by the imperfections of society. But instead of regarding culture as one of the givens in the relationship of nature and nurture, we now must ask, "What must a culture do to survive?" and "How can a culture be changed to increase its chances for survival?" In the ensuing dialog, we make the assumption that survival is desirable and that attempts to promote the widespread acceptance of that view are desirable. We will state as a premise that the promotion of a culture that increases the chances of individuals to develop as human beings has the best chances of survival, but that this cannot occur in less than several generations.

The question of "What must a culture do to survive?" has been approached tangentially by Daniel Callahan[12] in connection with a discussion of the ethical problems raised by the rapid "progress" made by the life sciences impinging on the practice of medicine. Callahan refers to culture as a "nurturing context, feeding and shaping us." He suggests that our culture is not really occupied with the questions "What is man?" "What is the good life?" "What is really harmful and what is really beneficial?" and he correctly, it seems to me, suggests that one function of a culture is to make up for our deficiencies in private wisdom, to allow us to know things with our feelings which we do not by philosophical standards know in our heads. Callahan calls for a resolution of the troubled relationship between ethics and the life sciences, but he concludes that this resolution must occur at the cultural level, not at the individual level. "To build a fresh ethic for the life sciences is to build a culture."[13] Thus he is led, as I have been, to the proposition that "To be viable, a culture must provide a nurturing ground for the development and enrichment of human life." Again: "Most critically, a culture will have to offer ways of meeting some basic human needs, needs which go beyond physical well-being."[14] His list has much in common with the properties I listed for an optimum environment (Table 1 in *Bioethics*[15]). His list

Table 1

A List of Human Needs as Derived from a Concept of Optimum Environment (from Potter,[15] pp. 144–145).

1. Basic needs: Food, shelter, clothing, space, privacy, leisure, education (moral and intellectual).
2. Freedom from toxic chemicals, unnecessary trauma, and preventable disease.
3. A culture having respect for sound ecologic principles.
4. A culture that prepares us for individual adaptive responses.
5. A sense of identity, with individual happiness that understands oscillations between satisfaction and dissatisfaction.
6. Productivity that involves commitment to other members of society.
7. An ongoing search for beauty and order that does not deny the role of individuality and disorder.

of human needs includes (1) a sense of meaning, (2) a sense of community, (3) a drive for values, (4) a drive for integrity, and (5) a drive for some kind of transcendence.[16] A somewhat similar list of human needs has also been proposed by Halleck, speaking as a psychiatrist also interested in the issue of survival (Table 2[17]). Callahan is primarily concerned with the development of an ethical system "capable of managing the issues thrown up by developments in the medical and life sciences," but it is clear that he believes that unless such a system (which I would call bioethics) is developed, our culture will not survive.

Table 2

A List of Human Needs (from Hallack,[17] pp. 203–235)

1. Intimacy	–with other people or a group
2. Influence	–attention, respect, affection
3. Freedom	–autonomy, dignity, individualism
4. Openness to Experience	–need for honesty
5. Action	–need for function
6. The Search for Meaning	–transcendence, purpose
7. Privacy	–as solitude, or as an adjunct to intimacy
8. Hope	–as concern for the future
9. Stability	–in relation to optimization of change
10. Non-violence	–in terms of the preservation of alternatives to violence

So what must our culture do to survive? According to Callahan, it must reach some kind of a consensus as to (1) the nature of man, what he is, and what he can become, (2) the extent to which nature (human and nonhuman) can and should be manipulated and controlled (the problem of intervention, see above), and (3) the relationship between public and private morality, law and ethics. Callahan wishes to be able to specify some fixed, normative human nature, by which one might test all proposals to cure, change, or improve man. "One could then say what is human, what is inhuman." As a beginning, he suggests that "man is a rational animal, *and* a culture-builder, *and* a tool-maker." Callahan's recurring use of the question as to "What is the normatively human?" and his reference to man as a rational animal are placed in a context that never considers the irrational aspects of nature and of human nature that I have emphasized: the tremendous diversity of human genetic characters; the disorder, randomness, and chance elements in every human genetic and environmental heritage. I agree with Callahan that "Some model of nature and man's relationship to nature stands behind every ethical system as well as specific ethical decisions." Callahan describes three models of the Man/Nature relationship, which I would paraphrase as (1) Man, The Master, dominating and overcoming nature, (2) Man, the steward over God's creation, and (3) Man, the student-philosopher, turning to nature and to his fellow men to build a culture that has survival and development as its goals.

Needless to say, my view favors the *third* model and has led to the advocacy of a culture that is based on bioethics as a normalizing world view. I believe that in order for a culture to survive it should encourage cultural pluralism in most areas, but it should avoid cultural laissez-faire. By this I mean that it should attempt to increase the understanding of the life sciences and life support systems by publicizing what we know and what we do not know, what we believe and what we do not believe, and why. We should attempt to increase the acceptance of honesty, of respect for human dignity and human needs, and of the fact that both nature and nurture combine to make each of us unique. We should recognize that none of us is completely rational all of the time, but that together we can be more rational about our irrational tendencies. I am convinced that it is wrong to assume with Locke that men have no inborn moral tendencies, but only a tendency to pursue pleasure and avoid pain.[18] I believe that natural selection has produced a much more complicated creature than this simplistic model would suggest, a creature that has firm bonds uniting him with nature in general and with his species in particular, a creature that feels instinctively an obligation to do something for his fellow creatures from day to day, and from this day to some distant tomorrow. This feeling is part of everyone's nature, mixed with and often overridden by other instincts and often overridden by ill-advised nurture. What we must do as concerned individuals is to strengthen those aspects of our culture that strengthen this instinctual morality.

Our culture must recognize the ties between humankind

and the plant and animal world. It must foster a morality with a goal that demands the preservation of the natural world, so that the human race can survive and develop further along paths that can be imagined today, but which have only a remote chance of being followed unless we change our course. It remains for a few concerned individuals to ask, "What *ought* the culture do to survive?" and "What *ought* some of us do to help develop such a culture?" The answer to the first question is relatively easy since it is clear that the preservation of diversity in individual human natures and nurtures is desirable, but this diversity should not be permitted to include life-styles that lead to irreversible damage to the natural world on which we all depend. The answer to the second question is much more difficult because it is unlikely that a mere continuation of every concerned individual simply doing his own thing is going to culminate in the kind of a culture that can survive. Right here, in this and in similar conferences, we ought to declare that the principle of maximizing cultural laissez-faire is bankrupt, even though we hold fast to an ideal of cultural pluralism. We ought to agree that some things are more important than others and begin to get on with the task of naming the important things and deciding how to get them woven into our culture.

Notes

1. Van Rensselaer Potter, *Bioethics: Bridge to the Future* (Englewood Cliffs, N.J.: Prentice-Hall, Inc., 1971).
2. Ernst Mayr, "The Nature of the Darwinian Revolution," *Science* 176 (June 2, 1972): 981–989.
3. T. S. Kuhn, *The Structure of Scientific Revolutions* (Chicago: University of Chicago Press, 1962).
4. Mayr, *op. cit.*, p. 981.
5. John Passmore, *The Perfectibility of Man* (New York: Charles Scribner's Sons, 1970), p. 9.
6. *Ibid.*, p. 149.
7. *Ibid.*, p. 169.
8. P. B. Medawar, *The Future of Man* (London: Methuen,

1960; New York: Basic Books, 1961), p. 53 in the Methuen edition.
9. Passmore, *op. cit.*, pp. 326–327.
10. R. Seidenberg, "Advertising and the Abuse of Drugs," *New England Medical Journal* 284 (1971):789.
11. Clifford Geertz, "The Impact of the Concept of Culture on the Concept of Man," in *New Views of the Nature of Man*, ed. John R. Platt (Chicago: University of Chicago Press, 1962), pp. 93–118.
12. Daniel Callahan, "Living with the New Biology," *Center Magazine* (July-August 1972):4–12.
13. *Ibid.*, p. 6.
14. *Ibid.*
15. Potter, *op. cit.*, pp. 144–145.
16. Callahan, *op. cit.*, p. 8.
17. Seymour L. Halleck, *The Politics of Therapy* (New York: Science House, Inc., 1971), pp. 203–235.
18. Passmore, *op. cit.*, p. 169.

Genetic Medicine: Notes on the Moral Literature

Richard A. McCormick, S.J.

Richard A. McCormick, S.J., of the Bellarmine School of Theology in Chicago, analyzes the moral literature re genetic medicine in terms of three methodologies that determine or influence ultimate attitudes and judgments: a consequentialist calculus, a more deontological attitude, and a "mediating" approach. He concludes with a personal reflection, in which he argues that the debiologizing of marriage and the family that is inherent in *in vitro* fertilization and cloning is depersonalizing and dehumanizing. Father McCormick's essay is from the September 1972 issue of the Jesuit publication *Theological Studies**—an issue that focused on "Genetic Science and Man" as its general theme. An associate editor of *America* and a past president of the American Catholic Theology Society, Father McCormick has contributed chapters to such volumes as *The Future of Ethics and Moral Theology*, *Norm and Context in Christian Ethics*, *All Things to All Men*, and *The Problem of Population.*

THE MORAL LITERATURE on genetic controls is enormous.[1] Furthermore, it touches on several different problems with ethical implications: eugenic engineering (both positive and negative), genetic counseling and screening, genetic abortion,[2] *in vitro* fertilization, cloning, etc. Much of the occasional writing is general in character.[3] The more systematic moral studies on genetics remind one of a masked ball: new disguises but behind them familiar faces. The familiar faces in this instance refer to the methodologies

* P.O. Box 1703, Baltimore, Md. 21203.

of well-known theologians on the (especially) American scene.

Hence, even in the face of the exciting and/or frightening possibilities of contemporary biomedicine, there is a lingering sense of *déjà vu* in the moral literature. Briefly, since ultimate attitudes and judgments vis-à-vis various genetic interventions depend heavily on how the author builds his approach, the emphasis falls heavily on methodology. Three approaches are discernible: a consequentialist calculus, a more deontological attitude, a "mediating" approach.[4]

Consequentialist Calculus

Joseph Fletcher, after reporting on some earlier writing on the subject,[5] sees the whole difference of opinion in terms of "apriorists" and "consequentialists."[6] This is, he says, "the rock-bottom issue . . . the definitive question in the ethical analysis of genetic control." The apriorists, relying on some kind of religious or nonempirical cognition, "would say, therefore, that therapeutic goals are not enough to justify *in virtro* fertilization, positive eugenics, or designed eugenic changes, no matter how desirable they might be." In contrast to this is a pragmatic or consequentialist ethics, which Fletcher claims as his own. "We reason from the data of each actual case or problem and then choose the course that offers an optimum or maximum of desirable consequences." Or again, "results are what counts and results are good when they contribute to human well being," a point to be situationally determined.

Fletcher then looks at a few cases and delivers his verdict. "I would vote for laboratory fertilization from donors to give a child to an infertile pair of spouses." As for cloning, Fletcher is a veritable cheerleader for the enthusiasts. "If the greatest good of the greatest number [i.e., the social good] were served by it," he would "vote" both for specializing the capacities of people by cloning and bioengineering parahumans or modified men. There then follows one of the most remarkable sentences in the contemporary literature on genetics: "I suspect I would favor making and using man-machine hybrids rather than genetically designed people for dull, unrewarding or dangerous roles needed nonetheless for the community's welfare—perhaps the testing of suspected pollution areas or the investigation of threatening volcanoes or snow-slides."[7]

Fletcher acknowledges several possible objections to all of this. First, it could be objected that since "fertilization or cloning result directly in human beings, or in creatures with nascent or protohuman status," the entailed practice of their sacrifice in the course of investigation is immoral. He dismisses this as "a priori metarational opinion," "belief in a faith assertion."

Having thus dismembered the first objection, he confronts the second, i.e., that there might be something inhuman about the laboratory reproduction of human beings. If one has a sneaking suspicion that behind Fletcher's enthusiasm there lurks a concept of "the human," he is absolutely right. "Man is a maker and a selector and a designer, and the more rationally contrived and deliberate anything is, the more human it is." This opens on a judgment which is at least competitive for "most remarkable statement of the year": "Laboratory reproduction is radically human compared to conception by ordinary heterosexual intercourse. It is willed, chosen, purposed and controlled, and surely these are among the traits that distinguish *Homo sapiens* from others in the animal genus, from the primates down. Coital reproduction is, therefore, less human than laboratory reproduction. . . ."[8]

To those who might object or hesitate, Fletcher has the reassuring word that "fear is at the bottom of this debate." But really we should fear not, for "to be men we must be in control. That is the first and last ethical word." Therefore, where cloning, donor insemination, etc., are concerned, "all this means that we are *going to have to change or alter* our old ideas about who or what a father is, or a mother, or a family."

Thus far Fletcher. I have cited him liberally because one has to, as it were, see it to believe it.

The time has come, I think, to blow the whistle on this type of thing. It is not a question of whether this genial Christian and gentlemanly ethician is right or wrong. We have all been a little bit of both, and much more of the latter. Rather, Fletcher continues to propose to do theology by setting up dubious polarities, promulgating unexamined premises, and flourishing rhetorical *non sequiturs*. The whole thing is then baptized into contemporary personalism with a now familiar ritualistic jargon: responsible, loving, pragmatic, personal. This is, of course, enormous fun; but it could be painfully expensive. If theologians are to retain any realistic hope of a dialogue with the scientific community, they must resolutely dissociate themselves from a type of discourse that too often dissolves into theology-by-anecdote.

First, the dubious polarities. An example is "apriorists vs. consequentialists." The former are accused of "religious, metaphysical, nonempirical" thought. They "would say, therefore, that therapeutic or corrective goals are not enough to justify *in vitro* fertilization, positive eugenics or designed genetic changes no matter how desirable they might be. . . . Good consequences could not, to the a priori moralist, justify such acts or procedures since they are wrong as means. . . ." Here Fletcher's typologies, while retaining a certain pedagogical utility, simply ignore the possibility that it is precisely a form of consequentialism that could lead to a rejection of these things. In other words, what some theologians are saying is that the very desirability of therapeutic or corrective goals is not an isolated factor but must be weighed in light of the personal and social costs involved in moving toward such goals. They are saying that *in vitro* fertilization, cloning, etc., no matter what long-term pragmatic advantages and reliefs they would seem to provide, reveal the decisive disadvantage of containing an attack on the *humanum*, and for this reason (or consequence) are to be avoided. This is hardly metarational apriorism.

Second, the unexamined premises. At the very time Fletcher tells us that the notion of humanness "may well be the most searching and fundamental problem that faces not only ethicists but society as a whole," he announces that the search is really over: "The more rationally contrived and deliberate anything is, the more human it is." This is at best ambiguous and at worst a distortion of the human. Rational control, it is true, is a distinctive achievement of man. But he can use this rationality in inhuman ways. Deliberation and rationality tell us only that a human being is acting, not that he is acting humanly. One can, with utter control and deliberateness, do the most monstrously inhuman things. The Third Reich showed us how. Theology has always known that sin, by definition, is a deliberate, rational, controlled choice—but the most inhuman of acts. Rational control, therefore, is not the guarantor of humane choices but only the condition of their possibility. What happens to man in and as a result of his rationality and deliberate choices tells us whether these choices were more or less human, more or less desirable.

Similarly, Fletcher has argued that "if the greatest good of the greatest number . . . were served by it," he would approve cloning, bioengineering of parahumans, etc. This remains an "unexamined premise" in several senses. (1) Have we not repeatedly experienced the fact that the greatest good of the greatest number, unassailable as it might be as a theoretical criterion, is practically the warrant for present practices and policies which all but guarantee that this greatest good will not be served? (2) How is the social good to be spelled out even if we accept it as a goal? Who makes the determination? On what basis? (3) How would laboratory reproduction, cloning, etc., serve it? True, Fletcher has said "if," but his failure to confront the serious, indeed decisive, problems buried in this "if" means that for him proportionate good too easily translates "anything to get the job done." He seems not to suspect that it just might be more human to exist with volcanic threats or pollution than to create parahumans to help us overcome these things. It is possible, after all, that by engineering the engineer we would become very competent barbarians. Not to raise such an issue is, in a sense, to have solved it. The editorial page of a subsequent issue of the prestigious *New England Journal of Medicine* carried a (by and large favorable) commentary on Fletcher by Bernard D. Davis, M.D.[9] At one point Davis notes: "One therefore wishes that Dr. Fletcher had discussed the conflicting interests and values that lie at the heart of ethical problems." Exactly.

Finally, the rhetorical *non sequiturs.* Fletcher informs us that in view of the new biomedical achievements "we are going to have to change or alter our old ideas about who or what a father is, or a mother, or a family." Here it must be said that we *have to* change these notions only if what *can* be done biomedically *ought* to be done humanly. Fletcher has given us no persuasive reasons why these things ought to be done, because he has not seriously examined what would happen to the doers in the process. For this reason his "have to change" is an unwitting but two-handed surrender to the scientific imperative. The contention here, then, is not precisely that Fletcher is a consequentialist, but rather that he has provided us with no grounds for thinking that he is a good one.

Deontological Attitude

Paul Ramsey and Leon Kass can be taken as examples of the second approach. The writings of Princeton's Ramsey are about as contrary to Fletcher as it is possible to be. If there is a practical issue in moral theology, chances are Ramsey has been there digging, sorting, and giving forth with his version of Christian wisdom ahead of the pack. There is, it can be said, hardly anyone who has not learned a good deal from him. It must also be said that there is hardly anyone who has not snapped at Ramsey's pedagogical hand in the process, a point verified by the recent literature on biomedicine.

Ramsey's weighing of the issues raised by the new biology draws heavily on two basic principles.[10] First, there is the "nature of human parenthood." Human parenthood demands that the spheres of procreation and marital love not be separated. This means that we may not procreate apart from the union of marital love, and that sexual love may not be expressed apart from a context of responsibility for procreation. Repeatedly Ramsey asserts that the inseparability of these two spheres is human parenthood "as it came to us from the Creator,"[11] that we dare not put asunder "what God joined together in creation."[12] On this score alone he rejects AID (donor insemination), cloning, reproduction *in vitro*.[13]

His second basic principle concerns the difference between therapy and experimentation. It might be formulated as follows: we may never submit another human being to experimental procedures to which he cannot consent when these procedures have no relation to his own treatment. On this basis, Ramsey believes that we could never *morally* get to know how to do certain things (e.g., cloning) because the very first attempt would have the character of an experiment on the child-to-be. Thus he says:

> Because we ought not to choose for a child—whose procreation we are contemplating—the injury he may bear, there is no way by which we can *morally* get to know whether many things now planned are technically feasible or not. We need not ask whether we should clone a man or not, or what use is to be made of frozen semen or ovum banks, or what sort of life we ought to create in hatcheries etc. since we can *begin* to perfect these techniques in no other way than by subjecting another human being to risks to which he cannot consent as our coadventurer in promoting medical or scientific "progress."[14]

Similarly, it is the distinction between therapy and experimentation that governs Ramsey's whole treatment of genetic surgery. Such treatment on an existing child, however drastic, is permissible if it does "not place the child at greater risk than now surrounds him as one of a specially endangered population." Here we are dealing with therapy. Where there is question, however, of an as yet unconceived child, Ramsey is rightly much more demanding. There would have to be *no discernible risks* in prospective genetic surgery before one could procreate a child likely to be burdened with Huntington's chorea, PKU, amaurotic idiocy, etc. Until such time as corrective genetic surgery is risk-free, the proper prevention of these diseases is "continence, not getting married to a particular person, not having any children, using three contraceptives at once, or sterilization." Any other procedure would be tantamount to illicit experimentation with human beings. Ramsey's study constantly returns to these two basic principles.

Ramsey's analysis is well informed, precise, and searching, even if frequently repetitious. Furthermore, one wishes that he were more successful in resisting the titillations of his own obiter dicta and neologisms. These more purple than persuasive asides simply blunt his theological punches. This being said, I would say that I find myself very close to nearly all of Ramsey's value judgments.[15] For this reason, it is all the more important to raise several issues which seem to call for further attention.

First, there is the manner of argument where Ramsey's two controlling principles are concerned. The first (the nature of parenthood as involving inseparability of the two spheres of love and procreation) he views as parenthood "as it comes to us from the Creator." He draws upon the Prologue of St. John and Ephesians 5 as loci where this divine plan is made clear.

The Prologue of John's gospel (not Genesis) is the Christian story of creation which provides the source and standard for responsible procreation, even as Ephesians 5 contains the ultimate reference for the meaning and nature of conjugal love and the standard governing covenants of marriage. Since these two passages point to one and the same Lord—the lord who presides over procreation as well as the lord of all marital covenants—the two aspects of sexuality belong together.[16]

Ramsey contrasts this nature-of-parenthood perspective with a method which would weigh AID (etc.) in terms of consequences.

Perhaps Ramsey is right. But the question can be raised whether the two approaches are that different, a point suggested in the discussion of Fletcher's work. Ramsey is equivalently saying that there are some principles which hold no matter what the consequences. Others might argue that the principles have been arrived at and do indeed hold precisely because of the intolerable consequences. Specifically, Ramsey seems to say that the two spheres of sexuality are inseparable because God made them this way and told us so. Others would say that they are inseparable because to separate them would dehumanize us, and *for this reason* we may say that God has joined them. It seems to me that Ramsey is not clear on how he derives this principle (and therefore, by implication, other principles). He seems to gather it from a reflective reading of Scripture and contrasts this with a consequentialist procedure. Yet over and over again he states it consequentially.

For instance, while discussing cloning, Ramsey states: "The conquest of evolution by setting sexual love and procreation radically asunder entails depersonalization in the extreme. The entire rationalization of procreation—its replacement by replication—can only mean the abolition of man's embodied personhood."[17] I agree, but is it not precisely because of these effects (alienation, depersonalization) that the statement is valid? We see more deeply into these things from John's Prologue and Ephesians 5, but the conclusion is not drawn independently of a consideration of effects or consequences, unless one has a very narrow notion of consequences.[18] Rather is it not precisely consequences which lead us to this conclusion? The dominating effect or consequence is the depersonalization of man, and this simply overrides any long-term eugenic goals. Therefore, it is far from clear that Ramsey should speak of his principle as valid independently of consequences.

To say that a certain procedure is depersonalizing or dehumanizing demands, of course, both some notion of the *humanum* and the predictable effects on the *humanum* of prospective procedures. I shall return to this shortly.

Ramsey's second principle (the immorality of experimentation without consent) raises a somewhat similar problem. In *The Patient as Person* he has argued—dealing explicitly with infants—that the reason for this conclusion is that such experimental procedures make an "object" of an individual. In these cases, he contends, the parents cannot consent for the individual. Consent is the heart of the matter. If the parents could legitimately consent for the child, then presumably experimental procedures would not make an object of the infant and would be permissible. Therefore, the basic question is: Why cannot the parents provide consent for the child? Why is their consent considered null here while it is accepted when procedures are therapeutic? To say that the child would be treated as an object does not answer this question; it presupposes the answer and announces it under this formulation.

Adults may donate an organ to another (*inter vivos*) precisely because their personal good is not to be conceived individualistically, but socially—that is, there is a natural order to other human persons which is in the very notion of the human personality itself. The personal being and good of an individual does have a relationship to the being and good of others, difficult as it may be to keep this in a balanced perspective. For this reason, an individual can become (in carefully delimited circumstances) more fully a person by donation of an organ; for by communicating to another of his very being he has more fully integrated himself into the mysterious unity between person and person.

Must not something analogous be said of experimentation for the good of others? It can be an affirmation of one's solidarity and Christian concern for others (through the advancement of medicine), though it is easy to be naive about the dangers and abuses of this idea. Becoming an experimental subject *can involve* any or all of three things: some degree of risk (at least of complications), pain, associated inconvenience (e.g., prolonging the hospital stay, delaying recovery, etc.). To accept these for the good of others could be an act of charitable concern.

If these reflections are true of adults, must not the same be said of infants and children in so far as they are human persons? Therefore, precisely why is parental consent illegitimate in their case? Or perhaps more sharply, the parents' consent to therapy directed at the child's own good is both required and sufficient because it is the closest we can come to a *reasonable presumption of the child's wishes.* The fact that the therapy or surgery is for the child's good could be but a single example of a reasonable presumption of the child's wishes. Are there others? According to Ramsey, no. But I wonder.

Perhaps the following approach is not totally without merit. It was suggested that organ donation and participation in experimentation (both within limits) could contribute to the personal good of the individual involved if his personal good is defined within its proper social setting. This is a general and abstract statement. It must be concretized and qualified.

The first qualification is that whether it is personally good for an individual to donate an organ or participate in experimentation is a very circumstantial and highly individual affair. For some individuals these undertakings could be or prove to be humanly destructive. Much depends on their personalities, backgrounds, maturity, present or future position in life, etc. The second and more important qualification is that these procedures become human goods for the donor or subject precisely because and therefore only when they are voluntary; for the personal good under discussion is the good of expressed charity. For these two reasons, I would conclude that no one else can make such decisions for an individual, i.e., *reasonably* presume his consent. He has a right to make them for himself.

But are there situations where such considerations are not involved and where the presumption of consent is reasonable? I think it is quite possible. For instance, if the only way a young child could be saved were by a blood transfusion from another child, I suspect that few would find such blood donation an unreasonable presumption on the child's wishes. The reason for the reasonableness of the presumption is not precisely that the blood donation is in any way a good for the donor. Rather it is that a great good is provided for another at almost no cost to the child. *Parum pro nihilo reputatur.* Could the same reasoning apply to experimentation? Concretely, when a particular experiment would involve no discernible risks, no notable pain, no notable inconvenience, and yet hold promise of considerable benefit, would not parental consent be a reasonable presumption of the child's wishes—not because it is in any way for the child's good, but because it is not in any realistic way to his harm? *Parum pro nihilo reputatur.* This is certainly to "use" the child, but in a way in which it is reasonable to presume he would want to be used, or not object to being used.

But we may not stop here. Since the individual has the right to make for himself decisions which involve risk, or pain, or notable inconvenience—a right which invalidates any presumption of his wishes—then he has a right to be protected against any possible violations of such a right, any dangers to it. It is here that one might argue the possible absoluteness of the personal-consent requirement. That is, our times are times of eager scientific research, enthusiastic eugenic ambitions, strong if subtle collectivistic tendencies, and growing impersonalization of health care. Thus it could be argued that we have a cultural situation with a built-in escalatory tendency to expose nonconsenting persons to violations of their rights. This means that there is a real danger of exceeding those limits to which the infant (e.g.) could be *reasonably* presumed to consent. He has a right to be protected against such a danger.

This danger is not sufficiently removed, it could be further argued, by the protections of parental consent, because this consent itself is in our day too often unstable and vulnerable to many noxious influences. Therefore, putting the nonconsenting person simply out of bounds where pure experimentation is concerned *might* be the only way to hold the delicate relation of individual to society in proper balance. I say "might" because if these dangers could be countered, then it would seem that some experimentation might be a reasonable presumption of the child's consent. If so, then this reasonableness would provide the basis for validating parental consent.

At this point, it must be said parenthetically that in these matters it is always better to err, if err one must, on the side of conservatism. Hence if there is any doubt about the reasonableness of the presumption or, more basically, about the validity of these reflections, the personal-consent requirement should be viewed as a practical absolute. More specifically, whether there is any risk, pain, or inconvenience involved is a matter which cannot be left exclusively in the hands of medical researchers. The terrible examples in M. H. Pappworth's *Human Guinea Pigs* make this clear. Some of the researchers regard as "trivial" or "routine" procedures the ordinary patient would, with good reason, view as seriously bothersome and notably risky. Because a complication can be handled by subsequent therapy does not mean it is no longer a complication. Medical technology can dazzle us into distorted human judgments.

The approach proposed here moves away a bit from the absoluteness of Ramsey's analysis, though not necessarily from the absoluteness of his conclusions. Ramsey's analysis must conclude that *any* experimentation, even the most trifling and insignificant such as a buccal smear, on nonconsenting persons is beyond the reach of parental consent because it involves us in "treating another as an object." Perhaps. But this latter seems to be a rhetorical way of formulating a judgment concluded on other grounds.[19] I have suggested that we might approach the morality of risk-free, pain-free, inconvenience-free experimentation, rare as such experiments might be, through the notion of reasonable presumption of the child's wishes. In other words, is it not possible that the inviolability against all experimentation (if we ought to maintain such inviolability) of those incapable of consent is only a relatively necessary conclusion of human prudence rather than of intrinsic morality? At least, I believe the question must be examined further.

The writings of Leon Kass reveal moral tendencies and judgments very close to those of Ramsey. For this reason, he would probably fall into Fletcher's apriorist pigeonhole. In his major writings Kass realistically limits himself to the two questions which have some practicality in the future: *in vitro* fertilization (with eventual uterine implantation) and cloning.[20]

As for the first, its least controversial use will be the provision of their own child to a sterile couple. At first glance, the intramarital use of artificial fertilization seems to resemble ethically AIH (artificial insemination by husband). But Kass raises two moral objections. First, the implantation of the embryo fertilized *in vitro* involves the hazards of deformity and malformation. These hazards are being imposed nontherapeutically on a child-to-be without his consent. This, Kass argues, "provides a powerful moral objection sufficient to rebut the implantation experiments." Secondly, discarding unimplanted embryos raises another problem. Kass is undecided as to whether we are dealing with a protectable humanity at this (blastocyst) stage, but we certainly will be at a later stage and therefore "had better force the question now and draw whatever lines need to be drawn." Apart from these objections, Kass finds no *intrinsic* reason to reject *in vitro* fertilization and implantation. But the argument must not stop here. A procedure possibly unobjectionable in itself makes possible other procedures. This is not an "argument from abuse." Rather he insists on

the fact that one technical advance makes possible the next and in more than one respect. The first serves as a precedent for the second, the second for the third—not just technologically but also in moral arguments. At least one good humanitarian reason can be found to justify each step. Into the solemn and hallowed tent of human sexuality and procreation, the camel's nose has led the camel's neck and may some day soon, perhaps, even lead the camel's spermatozoa.[21]

I suspect that Pius XII had something like this in mind when he condemned AIH.

As for cloning, Kass again raises the twin issues of production and disposition of defectives and contends with Ramsey that they "provide sufficient moral grounds for rebutting any first attempt to clone a man." He further urges the serious psychological problems of identity and individuality and finds them "sufficient to reject even the first attempts at human cloning."[22]

Kass eventually goes beyond this piece-by-piece approach and brings a broader cultural analysis to bear on the two questions. Here his writing is most powerful and persuasive. He argues that "increasing control over the product is purchased by the increasing depersonalization of the process" and that this depersonalization is dehumanizing. Against Fletcher's contentions he would insist that "human procreation is not simply an activity of our rational wills . . . it is more complete human activity precisely because it engages us bodily and spiritually, as well as rationally."[23]

The separation of reproduction from human sexuality Kass sees as a dehumanizing threat to the existence of marriage and the human family. "Transfer of procreation to the laboratory undermines the justification and support which biological parenthood gives to the monogamous (or even polygamous) marriage. Cloning adds an additional, more specific, and more fundamental threat: the technique renders males obsolete. All it requires are human eggs, nuclei, and (for the time being) uteri; all three can be supplied by women."[24]

Kass's concern for the family is not blind institutionalism. Rather he is concerned that "the family is rapidly becoming the only institution in an increasingly impersonal world where each person is loved not for what he does or makes, but simply because he is. The family is also the institution where most of us, both as children and as parents, acquire a sense of continuity with the past and a sense of commitment to the future."[25] For these and other reasons, Kass urges that "when we lack sufficient wisdom to do, wisdom consists in not doing." He is sharply critical of theologians-turned-technocrats (e.g., Karl Rahner[26]) whose notion of man as "freedom-event" provides no standards by which to measure whether self-modifying changes are in fact improvements.

Those unfamiliar with Kass will find his writings both enlightening and entertaining. Charles Stinson of Dartmouth College demurs.[27] He takes a rather dim view of the attitudes and analyses of Ramsey-Kass. He sees both of them as biomedical pessimists. Behind Kass's pessimism he finds a body-soul dualism, which contends: if mental-spiritual life is not a "separate entity" beyond genetic manipulation, it is somehow not as true as we had thought. Behind Ramsey's outlook, Stinson sees a faulty theology of creation "which assumes that God *intended* certain aspects of natural structures and forces to remain *always* beyond the control of man's intelligence." Stinson then repeats in a variety of ways what he mistakenly takes to be a counterstatement to Ramsey-Kass: increased empirical knowledge about the processes of life need not erode its divine meaningfulness. On the basis of such general assertions and the conviction that sooner or later we will be involved in "the socially regulated cloning of individuals," Stinson opts for the Rahnerian view that man's limitless power to experiment on himself is really a sign of the creaturely freedom given him by God.

Granted that the writings of both Ramsey and Kass do at times achieve liturgical fervor and leave them vulnerable to the accusation of both overstatement and pessimism, still Stinson's essay, interesting as it is, meets the serious issues they raise with little more than a gathering of evasions and begged questions.

Item. "No doubt, as Ramsey points out, accidental miscalculations and ignorance of variables will result in fetal monstrosities. Not a pretty picture to contemplate. Moreover, there will inevitably be abuses of power on the part of a small minority of insensitive or rash scientists and technicians. But are we to conclude that, because of its *risks* and possible abuses, all such work is intrinsically immoral?"[28] Since when is the certain ("no doubt") production of fetal monstrosities reducible to a mere risk? Ramsey may be wrong, but to talk of bench-made monstrosities as "risks" is hardly a persuasive way of showing it.

Item. "Ramsey's outlook is grounded . . . in a faulty theology of creation which assumes that God *intended* certain aspects of natural structures and forces to remain *always* beyond the control of man's intelligence."[29] Ramsey claims nothing of the kind. He does, indeed, argue (not "assume") that God intended certain aspects of natural structures as permanent, but he would insist that this is not to put them "beyond the control of man's intelligence"; it is only to say that certain controls may not be intelligent.

Item. "And why would a cloned human being not feel himself (or herself) to be a 'person' or 'embodied'? Possibly for a number of reasons, but Ramsey does not specify any."[30] To which, two things must be said. First, when Ramsey refers to cloning as involving "the abolition of embodied personhood," he need not and does not refer primarily to the feelings of the cloned product, but to the parents and their concept of parenthood. Secondly, he does indeed with Kass specify reasons about the feelings of the cloned human being.[31]

Item. "Let me hazard a key theological concept for the future: it is the ongoing content of human life that is spiritually significant—not its origin whether natural or artificial."[32] Comment: it is precisely the Ramsey-Kass point that artificial origin will affect the "ongoing content of human life." One must wrestle with this contention if one is to meet Ramsey-Kass where they are.

Item. "This feat [the first cloning of a man] would certainly not invalidate Ramsey's ethical norms but it would make them irrelevant speculatively."[33] Does the first use of the atomic bomb make it speculatively irrelevant to urge the question "Should we ever have done it?" If such a question is utterly urgent—as it is—then the more urgent question was: Should we do it? Our mistakes of the past should teach us at least to take these earlier questions more seriously—unless one wants to hold the disastrous view that we can learn only from our mistakes.

Item. Of genetics a hundred years hence, Stinson notes: "And this will *no doubt* include the socially regulated cloning of individuals who are deemed to be especially valuable to the community."[34] Here, I believe, is the real and ultimate pessimism: that because we *can* we certainly *will* do. Is there a better way to render any present ethical reflection irrelevant than to think it really makes no difference anyway, and therefore to reduce the issue to "what shall we do after we have cloned men?"

Mediating Approach

James Gustafson and Charles Curran are examples of the third approach. A methodology midway between the rather structureless utilitarian calculus of Fletcher and the Ramsey-Kass insistence on the absolute immorality of some means is that of Gustafson. Under a nine-point division, Gustafson lays out the many ethical issues in biomedicine.[35] Repeatedly, he sets up groups of alternative approaches, states the warrants for them, unravels their latent presuppositions, and notes the questions they raise.

For instance, in perhaps the most substantive sections of his study, Gustafson approaches genetic medicine from the contrasting positions of inviolable individual rights and the benefits which might accrue to others and society in general. He proposes three contrasting options. (1) The rights of individuals are sacred and primary, and therefore under no circumstances are they to be violated in favor of benefits to others. (2) Anticipated consequences judged in terms of the "good" that will be achieved or the "evil" avoided ought to determine policy and action regardless of the restrictions on individual rights that this might require. (3) Both 1 and 2 are one-sided. Decisions require consideration both of individual rights and of benefits to others. One of the two will be the base line, the other will function as the principle justifying exceptions to the base line.

It is clear that Gustafson would opt for the third alternative, indeed for third alternatives in nearly every case where opposing methods or stances have been proposed. Thus, as between "restricting the kinds of experimentation that will be permitted through civil legislation . . . and clearly defined moral rules" and "ensuring the maximum possible freedom for research," Gustafson goes for a bit of both: maintaining maximum possible freedom, but at the same time formulating principles and values which provide guidelines for procedures and for the uses of research. Similarly, he values summary rules, but is uncomfortable with absolute rules. Or again, he argues that "the value of human physical life is primary," but this does not "entail that no other values or rights might override the right to bodily life." He wants societal benefits to count in genetic decisions, but not at all costs, just as he wants individual rights to be respected, but not at all costs. And so on.

What I believe Gustafson is doing is trying to hold in balance or bring to terms two intransigent elements of moral discourse: the complexity of reality, yet the abiding need to attempt to bring our decisions under objective rational scrutiny if our moral policies are to remain truly human. These two elements constantly surface as Gustafson's profound concerns. Equivalently, he is suggesting that moral reasoning is neither as fixed and rational as Ramsey would sometimes lead us to believe, nor as shapeless and arbitrary as Fletcher's writing suggests.

Where does this leave him? With a goal and a means to it. The goal is the counsel that for man the experimenter and intervener "the chief task is to develop with both sensitivity and clarity an understanding of the qualities or values of human life and a conception of the basic human rights that will provide the moral guidelines or touchstones for human development."[36] That is why Gustafson's recent work has been concerned with the "normatively human." The means: ongoing, rigorous conversation between those who best pose ethical questions and those who are shaping developments in the biomedical field.

Gustafson's study—subtle, sensitive, sophisticated—resolutely avoids the blandishments of the shock statement and asks all the right questions. But there is one aspect of his approach which seems at least incomplete, even dissatisfying. For instance, he states that while the right to physical life is primary, "this would not entail that no other values or rights might ever override the rights to bodily life. . . ." Thus he endorses an "ordering which gives *some* guidance in particular decisions." Precisely at this point, it is necessary to say what these other values and rights might be and why they may be said to override the primary right.

Similarly, in dealing with biomedical procedures, Gustafson says that both individual rights and societal benefits must be considered. One of the two is the base line; the other functions as a principle justifying exceptions. Thus he says: "It might well be that under certain circumstances it is morally responsible to make the thrust of individual rights the base line, and under other circumstances the accounting of benefits." What are these circumstances? What is the criterion to make individual rights decisive in some instances, social benefits decisive in others? Until we know this, Gustafson's middle position is incomplete and fails to provide even "some guidance." It represents more a rejection of the opposing alternatives than a satisfying synthesis of the two.

This point should be urged because of its further implications. Let me put it this way. To say that there are overriding values *without stating what they might be*, to state that there are circumstances in which the base-line priority shifts *without stating what they might be*, is to do two things: (1) to empty the notions of "primary" and "base line" of most of their significance for decision-making; (2) to suggest that these overriding values can only be discovered in individual decision. I do not think that these are true. What Gustafson wants (and rightly) to say is that rational moral discourse is limited, that there comes a point when the complexity of reality leads us beyond the formulations of traditional wisdom. That, I think, is true. And I believe that we have always known it, even though we have not always admitted it. But where that point is located is very important. Failure to specify at least some of the values which can override a primary value or right all too easily suggests that there is no point to which rational deliberation can lead us, that we cannot specify these values, and that this can only be done in individual decisions. Does this not remove moral discourse in principle from objective and rational scrutiny? Gustafson does not want this, not at all. But how his admirable pastoral[37] sensitivities do not find their way to this theological cul-de-sac I fail to see.

I urge this point with a fear and trembling born of unqualified admiration for Gustafson's remarkable talents and work, of fear that the question may reflect my own overrationalization of the moral life, of the conviction that he as well as, and probably better than, any theological ethician on the American scene can bring light to those aspects of these remarks which hover in darkness.

Charles Curran states that moral theology, in facing biomedical problems, must proceed from a historical point of view, emphasize the societal aspects of the issues, and accept the self-creative power as a gift of equal importance with creatureliness.[38]

As for historical consciousness, we need a more "open" concept of man. For example, where Ramsey rejects Muller's eugenic proposals because they separate procreation and marital love, Curran agrees, but believes that "the teaching Ramsey finds in Ephesians 5 might also be historically conditioned."

Similarly, in the past we were guilty of an individualist reading of the principle of totality. The task of contemporary moralists is to do justice to the social, cosmic aspects of man without falling into collectivism. Contemporary genetic possibilities force on us a realization of responsibilities beyond the individual.

Thirdly, where the question of man's dominion is concerned, we must hold in tension man's greatness and creatureliness. Curran does not believe that Ramsey grants man enough dominion, just as he would believe that Fletcher uncritically grants him too much. Ramsey's one-sidedness Curran traces to an eschatology developed only in terms of apocalypse (discontinuity between this world and the next). Eschatology, Curran insists, must include three elements: the apocalyptical, prophetic, and teleological. After shaking and mixing these three ingredients, he ends with an eschatology where man's final stage is not totally continuous with man's present existence (against the utopians) and not totally discontinuous with it (against the apocalyptic likes of Ramsey).

On the basis of these broad strokes, Curran emerges with a position which states on the one hand that "there are important human values which would stand in the way of the geneticist on some occasions" (e.g., adhering to the bond between procreation and marital union), on the other that "one can envision certain historical situations in which *it might be sacrificed for greater values.*"[39]

The italicized words are interesting, for they indicate two things: (1) that Curran's basic position is very close to that of Ramsey and Kass; (2) that it is held on consequentialist grounds. This latter seems clear even against Curran's explicit denial, because if a value is "sacrificed for greater values," clearly a calculus model is operative. This leads one to force a question on Curran which his essay does not satisfactorily answer: *Why* hold in the first place that the spheres of procreation and marital love must in our historical time be held together? Ramsey gets this from a reflective reading of Scripture, the kind of argument Curran would reject as ahistorical and eventually deontological. Yet he also rejects the more experiential (consequentialist) model. What is left?

Curran's essay, like Gustafson's, is a helpful "both-and" balancing act, but at a different level—the level of broad cultural contrasts (e.g., between the narrowly scientific and the fully human, the utopian and the pessimistic, etc.). Ultimately, however, it finesses several of the hard questions and is less than complete in analyzing its own methodological presuppositions.

Thus far some recent moral literature; now to a concluding personal reflection. The two most commonly discussed issues seem to be fertilization *in vitro* and cloning.[40] The first is almost upon us and the second is possibly only decades away, though expert opinion differs about this. Furthermore, many of the moral issues in the more distant and exotic possibilities are essentially present in these problems. In both instances, Ramsey and Kass have seen a serious issue in the production and destruction of embryos. I do too, though I am not certain of the exact way the issue should be formulated. But given the cultural attitudes now prevalent toward fetal life, I have little confidence that these points will be taken very seriously by most biotechnicians. In one sense, of course, this is all the more reason for raising them. However, because the discussion surrounding production and disposition of the "failures" to some extent suggests that in other respects we should go ahead and that "artificial children" are desirable if these objections can be met, the more basic moral issue strikes earlier. It is that of marriage and the family.

Briefly, I am in deep sympathy with the views of Ramsey-Kass and (less explicitly) Curran that these procedures are inimical to marriage and the family (Ramsey says the "nature of parenthood") and that therefore in terms of their immediate implications and foreseeable effects we should not take such steps (nor *allow* them to be taken, since a public good of the first order is involved) unless a value the equivalent of survival demands it.

If there is, among the eugenic dreams and apocalyptic fears surrounding biomedical technology, a single certainty, it is this: *in vitro* fertilization and cloning do factually debiologize marriage and the family. Ramsey and Kass have argued that this is depersonalizing and dehumanizing. I believe they are right, and for two reasons.

First, by removing the origin of the child from the sphere of specifically marital (bodily, sexual) love, that love itself is subtly redefined in a way which deflates the sexual and bodily and its pertinence to human love, and therefore to the human itself. The artificially produced child can obviously be the result of a loving decision, even a deeply loving one; just as obviously it can be loved, cared for, and protected within the family. And precisely for these reasons it is quite valid to say that this child is the "product of marital love." But at this point, that term has undergone a change, a change which has to some extent debiologized and "debodified" the word "marital." The term has moved a step away from its full bodily and therefore *human* connotations. Man is everything we say of him: freedom, reason, body, emotions. He is the sum of his parts. To reduce his humanity to any one of these or, what is the same, to suppress any one of these from his humanity is dehumanizing. And that is what is happening here.[41]

Secondly, moving procreation into the laboratory "undermines the justification and support which biological parenthood gives to the monogamous marriage," as Kass puts it. In other words, the family as we know it is basically (not exclusively or eminently) a biological unit. To weaken the biological link is to untie the family at its root and therefore to undermine it. That this is dehumanizing and depersonalizing depends entirely on what one thinks of the family (or Kass's monogamous marriage).

The family, I would argue, embodies the ordinary conditions wherein we (parents, children, and others) learn to become persons. In the stable, permanent man-woman relationship, we possess the chance to bring libido and eros to the maturity of *philia*-friendship. Through monogamous marriage we experience the basic (not the only) form of human love and caring, and learn thereby to take gradual possession of our own capacity to relate in love. That is why marriage is a sacrament: it is the human stuff eminently capable of mirroring God's own covenant-fidelity, His love. It is the ordinary societal condition of our coming to learn about responsibility, tenderness, fidelity, patience, the meaning of our own sexuality, etc. Without its nourishing presence in our midst, we gamble with our best hope for growth and dignity, our chances of learning what it means to love and be loved. For those created by and in the image of a loving God, and therefore destined to a consummation in this image, such a gamble is humanly suicidal. To undermine the family in any way would be to compromise the ordinary conditions of our own growth as persons, and that is dehumanizing.

Obviously, marriages (and families) fail. And just as obviously, the surrogate arrangements which pick up the pieces of our weakness, failure, and irresponsibility can and do succeed. Furthermore, it seems undeniable that the contemporary shape of family life cries out for restructuring if monogamous marriage is to survive, grow, and realize its true potential. But these facts do not negate the basic necessity of the monogamously structured family for human growth. They only say that it is worth criticizing vigorously because it is worth saving.

These reflections are not likely to be very persuasive to a culture which, it can be argued, is comfort-bent, goal-oriented, technologically sophisticated, sexually trivialized, and deeply secularized. But if they are true, they suggest that the moral theological analysis of the biomedical problems discussed in these pages must attend much more than it has to a Christian critique of the culture which not only generates such remarkable possibilities, but above all shapes our reflection about them.[42]

Notes

1. Literature of the 1960's can be found in Rosalind P. Petchesky's *Issues in Biological Engineering*, ISHA Bulletin no. 7 (Institute for the Study of Science in Human Affairs; New York: Columbia Univ., 1969). Cf. also *Theological Studies* 30 (1969):680–92, where I review the recent periodical literature. This literature will not be reviewed here. Another valuable bibliographical source is Sharmon Sollitto's "In the Literature," which appears regularly in the *Report* of the Hastings Center.
2. A conference at Airlie House, Va. (Oct. 10–14, 1971) was devoted to "Ethical Issues in Genetic Counselling and the Use of Genetic Knowledge." It dealt heavily with counseling, screening, and abortion. The papers, currently in the process of publication, include thoughtful essays by Daniel Callahan, Paul Ramsey, James Gustafson, Leon Kass, and John Fletcher. For a brief report of this conference, cf. W. G. Peter, "Ethical Perspectives in the Use of Genetic Knowledge," *BioScience* 21 (Nov. 15, 1971): 1133–37.
3. Cf., e.g., Donald Huisingh, "Should Man Control His Genetic Future?" *Zygon* 4 (1969): 188–99; S. E. Luria, "Modern Biology: A Terrifying Power," *Nation* 209 (1969):406 ff.; Kenneth Vaux, "Cyborg, R. U. Human? Ethical Issues in Rebuilding Man," *Religion in Life* 39 (1970):187–92. Articles

of this kind abound in the medical journals and journals such as *Science* and *Science News*. Cf., e.g., *New York Times Magazine*, March 5, 1972, pp. 10 ff.

4. The very problems theologians decide to discuss are important, for a false move here could bring theology and its important contributions to biomedical decisions into disrepute with the scientific world. Furthermore, too great a futurism would allow existing problems to get solved by default. The matter is complicated by the fact that theologians are at the mercy of the scientific world in deciding what problems are realistic and this very world gives ambiguous answers. For instance, James D. Watson reports of Joshua Lederberg's attitude toward cloning that "to him, serious talk about cloning is essentially crying wolf when a tiger is already inside the walls" ("Moving toward the Clonal Man," *Atlantic*, May, 1971, p. 52). Many authors view cloning as too far into the future to merit serious discussion now. On the other hand, statements such as that of Bernard D. Davis, M.D., are not infrequent: "Cloning is thus the aspect of genetic intervention that most requires public discussion today" (*New England Journal of Medicine* 285 [1971]:800).
5. Inaccurately in at least several places. Speaking of "genetic engineering," Fletcher states that "Richard McCormick condemns it because, he believes, only monogamously married heterosexual reproduction is morally licit." The reference is to *Theological Studies* (cf. n. 1 above), where a position on "monogamously married heterosexual reproduction" is indeed endorsed; but this endorsement is far from a condemnation of all "genetic engineering," as even a quick reading will reveal. Similarly of Dr. Andre Hellegers, Fletcher writes: "A Catholic obstetrician . . . has complained that it is 'arbitrary' to start regarding a fetus as human at the 20th week or at 'viability,' and yet the physician himself insists on the even more arbitrary religious doctrine that a fertilized ovum before implantation is human." Fletcher has misread Hellegers' point (*Washington Post*, Jan. 9, 1971, p. A21). Hellegers was simply challenging the *Post*'s concern over test-tube babies, since that paper had for years supported the proposition that fetuses before the 20th week could be destroyed. If fetuses can be destroyed before this time, Hellegers rightly wonders why it is improper for scientists to create such blobs of tissue. The point is the *Post*'s consistency, nothing more.
6. Joseph Fletcher, "Ethical Aspects of Genetic Controls," *New England Journal of Medicnie* 285 (1971):776–83.
7. *Ibid.*, p. 779.
8. *Ibid.*, p. 781.
9. Cf. n. 4 above. For other reactions to Fletcher's article, cf. *New England Journal of Medicine* 286 (1972):48–50.
10. Paul Ramsey, *Fabricated Man* (New Haven: Yale Univ. Press, 1970).

11. *Ibid.*, p. 124.
12. *Ibid.*, p. 38.
13. Ramsey approves of AIH in a sterile marriage (p. 112). How this is consistent with his basic principle is somewhat hazy. He writes: "Their response to what God joined together . . . would be expressed by their resolve to hold *acts* of procreation . . . within the sphere of *acts* of conjugal love, within the covenant of marriage" (p. 36). AIH is certainly an act of procreation, and it is certainly within the covenant of marriage; but that it is "within the sphere of *acts* of conjugal love" is far from clear. Perhaps Ramsey stated his principle poorly here.
14. *Ibid.*, p. 134.
15. I say "nearly all" because I cannot agree with Ramsey that "we cannot rightfully *get to know* how to do this [use an artificial placenta] without conducting unethical experiments upon the unborn" (p. 113). If a pregnant woman with a non-viable fetus is dying and the only even remote hope of bringing her otherwise doomed child to term is an artificial placenta, I would think it legitimate—as therapy, not experimentation, or at least not exclusively experimentation.
16. *Ibid.*, p. 37.
17. *Ibid.*, p. 89. Ramsey reveals a similar approach in many places. For instance, on cloning, he says it would not be right "because of its massive assaults upon human freedom and its grave violation of the respect due to men and women now alive and to human parenthood as such" (p. 61). Again, speaking of the separation of procreation and marital love, he notes: "Herein men usurp dominion over the human—the dominion they hold rightfully only over the animals. This is bound to pierce the heart of the *humanum* in sex, marriage and generation" (p. 88).
18. By "consequences" I include two things: the immediate entailments or implications of an action, the more mediate aftereffects.
19. That Ramsey himself might agree with this and the underlying method is suggested by his attitude toward exceptional instances in situations of consent. He notes: "In the grave moral matters . . . a physician is more liable to make an error in moral judgment if he adopts a policy of holding himself open to the possibility that there may be significant, future permissions to ignore the principle of consent than he is if he holds this requirement of an informed consent always relevant and applicable" (*The Patient as Person* [New Haven: Yale Univ. Press, 1970], p. 9).
20. Leon Kass, "Making Babies—the New Biology and the 'Old' Morality," *The Public Interest*, Winter, 1972, pp. 18–56. This long study is nearly identical with Kass's "New Beginnings in Life," an occasional paper privately published by the Hastings Center (Institute of Society, Ethics and the Life Sciences). Cf. also Leon R. Kass, "The New Biology: What

Price Relieving Man's Estate?" *Science* 174 (1971):779–88, and his "What Price the Perfect Baby?" *Science* 173 (1971): 103–4.

21. "Making Babies," pp. 38–39. The last sentence of the citation occurs only in the earlier ("New Beginnings in Life") version. Either its frivolity annoyed the editor of *Public Interest* or Kass waxed formal when he went public.
22. *Ibid.*, p. 45.
23. *Ibid.*, pp. 48–49.
24. *Ibid.*, p. 50.
25. *Ibid.*, p. 51.
26. The reference to Rahner is to "Experiment: Man," *Theology Digest* 16 (1968):57–69. (Cf. "Experiment Mensch: Theologisches über die Selbstmanipulation des Menschen," *Schriften zur Theologie* 8 [Einsiedeln: Benziger, 1967], 260–85.) Rahner's position is not accurately presented if it is drawn from "Experiment: Man" alone. His "Zum Problem der genetischen Manipulation" (*Schriften zur Theologie* 8, 286–321) must also be read. In this latter essay Rahner develops positions very close to those of Ramsey and Kass and manifests a deep skepticism, even negativism, where eugenic genetic manipulation is concerned. He insists, e.g., that not everything that can be done ought to be done (p. 318). In applying this to donor insemination, Rahner argues that personal sexual love has an essential relationship to the child; for the child is the expression and realization of the abiding unity of the spouses. But "genetic manipulation does two things. First it separates on principle the procreation of a new person (as the abiding expression of the love-union of the spouses) from marital union. Secondly, it transfers procreation (sundered and separated from its human source) outside of the human sphere of intimacy" (p. 313). That Rahner would reject this is obvious. Furthermore, he speaks repeatedly of resisting "the temptation of the possible" and calls "immunity against the fascination of the newly possible" a virtue contemporary man must develop, and apply in the area of genetic manipulation. One of Rahner's major concerns is how his basic "No" to some of these possibilities can be made persuasive amid the existing moral pluralism. The Ramsey-Kass criticism of Rahner is, therefore, not only misleading in itself; it also *seems* to provide the support of a great theological name for utopian schemes and eugenic experiments which Rahner would resolutely disown.
27. Charles Stinson, "Theology and the Baron Frankenstein: Cloning and Beyond," *Christian Century* 89 (1972):60–63.
28. *Ibid.*, p. 60.
29. *Ibid.*, p. 61.
30. *Ibid.*
31. Cf. Ramsey, *Fabricated Man*, pp. 71–72.
32. *Art. cit.*, p. 63.
33. *Ibid.*, p. 62.

34. *Ibid.*
35. James M. Gustafson, "Basic Ethical Issues in the Bio-Medical Fields," *Soundings* 53 (1970):151–80.
36. *Ibid.*, p. 178.
37. I use the word "pastoral" because I wonder to what extent Gustafson is lifting the anguish of personal decision (to which, of course, it is all too easy to become insensitive) into the larger sphere of moral policy and general moral reasoning.
38. Charles Curran, "Theology and Genetics: A Multi-faceted Dialogue," *Journal of Ecumencial Studies* 7(1970):61–89. (This also appeared as "Moral Theology and Genetics" in *Cross Currents* 20 [1970]: 64–82.)
39. *Ibid.*, p. 83.
40. Though with regard to *in vitro* fertilization several variations must be weighed distinctly for their differences: (1) with husband's seed or donor's; (2) with implantation in wife's uterus or someone else's; (3) with no implantation but use of artificial placenta (etc.)—a development apparently rather far off. For differing views on *in vitro* fertilization, cf. *Medical-Moral Newsletter* 8 (March-April, 1972) entire issue, and *Hastings Center Report* 2 (1972):1–3.
41. Cf. Rahner, "Zum Problem der genetischen Manipulation," p. 313.
42. This bulletin was composed at and suported by the Kennedy Center for Bioethics, Georgetown University, Washington, D.C.

II. Life-Sequence

Shall We "Reproduce"?

Paul Ramsey

Noted ethicist Paul Ramsey is perhaps the leading spokesman for the view that the manipulation of embryos, or *in vitro* fertilization, constitutes unethical medical experimentation. In his opinion, such experimentation cannot be justified on the basis of the medical field's own moral standards, quite apart from any appeal to religious or other ethical criteria: "Either the accepted principles of medical ethics must give way, or fabricated babies should not be ventured." Initially presented as a paper at the International Symposium on Human Rights, Retardation, and Research, sponsored by the Joseph P. Kennedy, Jr., Foundation in Washington, D.C. on October 16, 1971, Dr. Ramsey's forcefully reasoned negative moral verdict on technological "reproduction" appeared as a two-part article in the *Journal of the American Medical Association* (June 5 and June 12, 1972).* Among his several books, two are particularly pertinent to this article: *Fabricated Man: The Ethics of Genetic Control* and *The Patient as Person: Explorations in Medical Ethics*. Dr. Ramsey is Harrington Spear Paine Professor of Religion at Princeton University.

* 535 North Dearborn St., Chicago, Ill. 60610.

I. The Medical Ethics of In Vitro Fertilization

I MUST JUDGE that in vitro fertilization constitutes unethical medical experimentation on possible future human beings, and therefore it is subject to absolute moral prohibition. I ask that my exact language be noted: I said, unethical experimentation on *possible future human beings*. By this, I mean the child-to-be, the "successful" experiments when they come.

I mean to exclude three things that could be said additionally to make a showing of medical immorality and a notation of illicitness upon the trials that are currently being performed. Excluded is (1) the charge that before going to human experimentation, physicians should not have omitted first proving their technique in species more closely related to man, on the primates, e.g., monkeys. This is a question of the background needed in the experimental design which an amateur cannot judge. Still I do know enough about discussions among ethical physicians concerning the need to complete the "animal work" before going to "human work" to know that this is a serious charge that requires some answer from the physicians attempting in vitro fertilization and implantation in human females—an answer which I have not seen. Excluded from my chief concern is also (2) the charge that the women "volunteers"—urged on as they are by a desperate desire to overcome their oviduct obstruction and to have a child of their own—have not given a fully understanding consent to what is being done upon them and by means of them. Clearly, the women already submitted to laparoscopy are experimental subjects, not patients who are likely to get children by this unproven technique. It is not enough to say to them, as Dr. Edwards is reported to have said, that "your only hope is to help us."[1] Now, I know that there is a spectrum and no clear lines to be drawn between pure experiment, therapeutic investigation, and proven therapy. Still, one way to make a significant distinction along this spectrum is to suppose one of these women to ask, "Doctor, are you doing this for *me* or am I doing it for you and your research?" The answer to that question to date is that the women are undergoing surgery and other procedures for the sake of medical research; and it is a cardinal principle of medical ethics that they should have knowingly consented to that, and not primarily to a therapy they hoped would relieve their own childlessness.

Excluded also from my present concern is (3) the charge that it is immoral to discard or terminate the lives of the zygotes, the developing cluster of cells, the blastocysts, the embryos, or the fetuses it will be necessary to kill in the course of developing this procedure. Persons who believe that an individual human life begins with conception or after the time of segmentation or at implantation or with the morphologically human fetus or with heartbeat or ECG readings or self-movement (or any time before birth) must regard experiments in in vitro fertilization and artificial implantation as ab initio inherently immoral, because the physician must be willing to discard mishaps at any point in that span of time which do not come up to the standards of an acceptable human being. Make no mistake about it, this will extend, through screening by amniocentesis and fetoscopy, well into the period in which hysterotomy would have to be done if a defective result is detected, in order to abort the wrong life begun in the laboratory. I have a great deal of sympathy for the conclusion that this is, therefore, a wrong way to begin a human life. Still, when I say that in vitro fertilization followed by implantation is an immoral experiment on possible future human beings, I do not assume any of these notions (for some of which there are better reasons than the socially prevailing notion) of when the possible future human being is an actual human being.

Instead, I assume the going perception of when there is a human life: when we see it before our eyes in the incubator, in a hospital nursery, in a bassinet or a playpen, playing hopscotch on the sidewalk, or going to kindergarten; and I assert that it clearly seems to me that in vitro fertilization followed by implantation is an immoral experiment on such a possible future human life.

Dr. Patrick Steptoe, Dr. Edwards' colleague, is reported[2] to have said that the decision to implant a given embryo, based on statistical evidence and hope—an embryo which cannot be karyotyped for genetic or other damage as a final procedure before implantation without too grave risk of further, more serious damage—will "call for a 'brave decision.'" Bravery, courage, used to be the word for a man's moral virtue in the face of danger or adversity. If (as I believe) we should watch our language as we watch our morals, Dr. Steptoe seriously misused language. What he meant was "rashness" in action regardless of the consequences to another human life, and not "courage," facing one's own perils or adversities. That, in former, more moral ages of mankind, was viewed as a vice.

Dr. Daniele Petrucci of the University of Bologna is a rather discredited pioneer among these adventurers. He is discredited, however, for not having published a scientific article; his experiment was "insufficiently documented"; other scientists could not repeat his procedures or check his results or even know his claims were not fraudulent. He was not discredited, however, for doing what he said he did to a human fetus; for what he might well have done to a possible future human life if his experiment had been continued or had that in view. In 1961 Petrucci reported that after more than forty failures he had successfully fertilized a human egg in vitro, cultured the embryo for twenty-nine days ("a heartbeat was discernible") and then destroyed it because "it became deformed and enlarged—a monstrosity." Nor, so far as I know, has Petrucci's end-in-view been generally excluded from among the possible purposes of manipulating embryos; indeed, one finds frequent mention of related designs in experimental biology: Petrucci told Italian newspapermen that he only meant to find a way to culture organs that would resist the rejection phenomenon when transplanted. With that, Petrucci yielded to his Church's condemnation of producing a human being without "the most supreme assistances of love, nature and conscience" (editorial, *L'Osservatore Romano*) and became a forgettable episode in the history of in vitro fertilization research—unless, while in Russia to receive a medal, he passed on his arts to experimental biologists there.[3]

My reason for bringing up the Petrucci episode is not, rhetorically and emotionally, to tar more responsible scientists with the damage he was willing to accept. It is rather to say simply that unless the *possibility* of such damage can be definitively excluded, in vitro fertilization is an immoral experiment on possible future human beings. And it is to say that this condition cannot be met, at least not by the first "successful" cases, and therefore that any man's or any woman's venture to begin human life in this way is morally forbidden. We cannot morally *get to know* how to perfect this technique to relieve human infertility (even if, once perfected, it would not be a disastrous further step toward the evil design of manufacturing of our posterity).

We all know from the popular and the scientific accounts that in order to accomplish in vitro fertilization, scientists must mimic nature perfectly.

The mammalian egg has been carefully adapted over many centuries of evolution and natural selection to a very delicate balanced environment in the ovarian follicle, the fallopian tube, and the womb. Likewise, the mammalian and human sperm has been adapted through millennia by natural selection to survive in the environment of the vaginal canal and the uterus and achieve fertilization in the fallopian tubes. . . . The scientist must duplicate almost exactly this delicately balanced internal environment of the female reproductive tract, or fail in his attempt to achieve in vitro fertilization.[4]

This artificial mimicry of nature has been accomplished in the matter of fertilization and the culture of human life until well beyond the time implantation would take place naturally. Along the way, the scientists have learned a great deal about duplicating the environment in which the sperm can be "capacitated"; they have learned that fertilization is not a "moment" but a process, that cells that seem to be fertilized may only be dying. (Claims to scientific fame depend on this latter point!)

The same can be said about those scientists who are at work assaulting and attempting to duplicate human gestation in the middle and later stages. They too must be able to mimic natural human gestation entirely; the slightest lapse or mistake would be disastrous to a possible future human being.

My point as an ethicist is that none of these researchers can *exclude* the possibility that they will do irreparable damage to the child-to-be. And my conclusion is that they cannot morally proceed to their first ostensibly successful achievement of the results they seek, since they cannot assuredly preclude all damage.

However much these experimental embryologists may have mimicked nature perfectly, they cannot guarantee that the last artificial procedure they carry out before implantation (or know they cannot carry through, such as karyotyping, which Dr. Steptoe cited when he erroneously spoke of "bravery") may be the important one. The last procedure may induce damage (or the last procedure known to be possibly damaging may not be able to be used although it might detect damage induced by previous procedures). Damage could be introduced during the transfer procedure, even after the last inspection is made. The last inspection may induce damage, or it may not be done because it could be fatal or damaging. For all we know, the manipulation may implant embryos that, if abnormal, will not be spontaneously aborted with the same frequency as under natural conditions. Finally, detectable natural abnormalities and detectable induced abnormalities may prove inseparable to such a degree that it will be difficult to establish exactly what are the additional risks due to this procedure. If true, that would be a limit upon experimental designs, even if one had gotten over the earlier objections that it is immoral to use the child-to-be to find out.

These are some of the reasons in vitro fertilization followed by implantation must necessarily require (by an amazing degradation of moral language) "courage" on the part of the physician-experimenter. He can never know what he is doing to a possible future human being. Even if he had not omitted experiments on monkeys first, no trial on monkeys would have told him whether he was or was not in the human case inducing mental retardation. It will not be enough to be able to discard grossly damaged embryos; there may well be damage that cannot be grossly scanned (as later on a club foot can be) and which are of crucial importance for the normal human capacity of the child-to-be. This is why experimentation on the primates could never settle the issue I am raising.

Anyone familiar with discussions of the ethics of medical experimentation knows that physicians acknowledge that the passage from "animal work" to work in the human always involves unknown risks that cannot have been tested before. Because of this fact, the move to human experimentation is made only when physicians secure the partnership of an informed, consenting volunteer for nonbeneficial investigation or when they already have a patient suffering from an illness, to cure which they need and he equally needs investigational therapy to be performed. They do not (or should not) first manipulate a patient's consent. Nor do they first manipulate a patient so that he is in some need of possibly harmful treatment. Neither of these two conditions for moving to "human work" can be met in the case of in vitro fertilization and embryo transfer. The child-to-be is not a volunteer; and before his beginning he is in no need of physicians to learn how not to harm him.

There are more cautious physicians and others who seem to believe that these obstacles and objections in the way of justifying in vitro fertilization will fall without the need for immoral experimentation on possible future human beings in the process. They have not, in my opinion, paid attention to the logic of the matter, to the unforeclosable risks involved in moving to the human work or to the necessity of bringing the first cases to term (and beyond) in order ever to learn whether the trial did harm or not. Thus, Dr. Kenneth Greet, a British Methodist, referring to criteria laid down some years ago by the British Council of Churches, stated:

> Provided the fertilization of the ovum is undertaken in order that it should be transplanted into the lining of the uterus, and provided also no harm is done at that stage which would result in malformation, then I think it is something to be welcomed.[5]

And Dr. Luigi Mastroianni, chairman of obstetrics and gynecology at the University of Pennsylvania, is reported[6] to have said:

> It is my feeling that we must be very sure we are able to produce normal young by this method in monkeys before we have the temerity to move ahead in the human. . . . In our laboratory, our position is, "Let's explore the thing thoroughly in monkeys and establish the risk." Then we can describe the risk to a patient and obtain truly informed consent before going ahead. We must be very careful to use patients well and not be presumptuous with human lives. We must not be just biologic technicians.[7]

Surely Dr. Mastroianni's very fine statement falls of its own weight. Because his is a splendidly articulated statement, it is clear that the conditions he lays down for not being "presumptuous with human lives" cannot be fulfilled (or that in the case of the woman's consent, they are not sufficient). One is apt to miss this when reading Dr. Greet's statement of the basic principle of medical ethics ("do no harm") which is not articulated for the case under consideration; he leaves wide open the possibility that the criteria can be met. While Dr. Mastroianni also seems to believe that this test can be met, his statement makes evident that it cannot. Work in monkeys would enable scientists to describe the risks accurately for monkeys, but not for possible deep injuries in the human case—for example, hemophilia or mental retardation or multifactoral personality and behavioral defects. These can be known only by work in humans, which, because the risks are not known, would be immoral to research by means of a possible case of embryo transplant brought to birth. Moreover, to be able to "describe the risk to a patient" (the woman, only) and to "obtain truly informed consent before going ahead" would relieve the physician of presumptuous manipulation of her consent. But that would in no way relieve the physician of complicity in such a woman's willingness to be "presumptuous" with a human life—her child-to-be—or from guilt for allowing her or enticing her to consent to any such thing, even if the risk could be exactly described from work in monkeys.

Is there any answer to this argument against in vitro fertilization—an argument which, I believe, must hold unless we are cloyed by the sentiment that a woman should be enabled to have a child by any means and if we are not simply fascinated by "advancements" in the scientific possibilities of unusual modes of human fecundity?

One answer is that after implantation, intrauterine monitoring by means of amniocentesis, or fetoscopy when it is developed, will enable physician-scientists to scan and screen their results, and by abortion discard their mishaps, i.e., any lives later discovered to have been damaged by the procedures of in vitro fertilization and implantation itself.

The proper reply to this retort is that invading the uterus to make these checkups may itself induce additional damage to the fetus, not only to the woman. Physicians engaged in amniocentesis usually concentrate on the statistical incidence of this possibility, which is low. One or two percent, they say, which in their practice is to be compared with a like statistical risk that the fetus already conceived may be defective in one way or another. That, I would say, is a different moral problem than if human ingenuity first creates at risk the human life which must thereafter be monitored, at those additional risks, by amniocentesis with abortion as the refuge in case it is discovered that one had seriously impaired the life he meant to produce. To monitor by amniocentesis a fetus already conceived and determined to be at special risk of being genetically damaged *may* be justified by balancing that unborn child's already existent 1% or 2% risk of genetic disease against the 1% or 2% of risk that the procedure to find out may itself do damage. But even if that is an ethical practice in medicine, the cases we are discussing—in vitro fertilization and artificial implantation—do not already have a patient at risk. The possible future human being is at risk only of being created in this way, of having someone wrongly accept for him an incidence of additional risk of induced damage from the procedure chosen to be used in his creation.

Then there are those physicians who go behind the equilibration of incidence of risk and speak frankly of the depth of what is at risk in every case in which amniocentesis is used. So we must add to the original "daring" venture to create a human life the additional risks, however small, of serious damage which monitoring what we had done itself imposes on a possible future human being. Henry Nadler, MD, of Children's Memorial Hospital, Chicago, refreshingly says that only defects established before amniocentesis is performed (12 weeks) can be excluded from its possible adverse effects.

> There is no way with present studies . . . of establishing ten or fifteen years from now if these children lose 5 or 10 IQ points. We might be able to get an approximation during the first year of life if their rate of growth is significantly different. However, more subtle damage will be difficult to evaluate.[8]

In short, if in vitro fertilization scientists appeal to intrauterine monitoring as an "out" after what they may have done by their last procedure (which by definition could not at that point be monitored), they may only be adding possible damage to possible damage that cannot be excluded and which may be brought upon a possible future human being whom they thus dare to initiate.

I see no line of moral reasoning that can justify this as an ethical practice of medicine. Nor do I see how any woman could *knowingly* consent to it. But, then, there may be depths I do not fathom in "Women's Lib"!

A negative moral verdict upon in vitro fertilization follows from right-ordered concern for the child that will be produced by the "successful" cases of these experiments. It is not a proper goal of medicine to enable women to have children and marriages to be fertile *by any means*—means which *may* bring hazard from the procedure, *any* additional hazard, upon the child not yet conceived. To suppose otherwise is to believe couples have such an absolute right to have children that this right cannot be overriden by the requirement that we should first have to exclude any incidence of *induced* risk to the child itself. This would be to adopt an extreme pronatalist assumption that an unconceived child somehow already has a title to be conceived. In such pronatalism, extremes meet: artificial modes of conception and gestation find themselves strange bedfellows with the insistence of a few uninstructed Roman Catholics that the life-giving potentiality of sperm and ovum are not artificially to be denied. (An illiterate spokesman for this point of view once told me that this was what Jesus meant when he said "Suffer the little ones to come unto me. . . !") Thus, the justification of in vitro fertilization and the prohibition of contraception both alike exalt—though in different ways—the absolute rights of "nature." The good of the possible future human being is not allowed, in the first case, to "interfere" with getting pregnant artificially, nor in the second case to interfere with natural fecundity.

The conclusion that a child should be conceived at risk of induced damage requires not only the assumption that while yet nothing, he somehow had title to be born (which, if true, might warrant our taking *his* risks in his behalf). In medical circles, this requires also the mind-boggling assumption that an unconceived child is somehow the equivalent of an existing child as already the subject of medical care and, therefore, a proper subject of investigational therapy without his consent. So only can we bring him under the ordinary categories and balancing judgments of medical treatment at risk. By first imagining the qualitative gulf separating being from nonbeing to have been traversed—and only so—can we imagine that proper treatment (of his being) means simply taking every precaution to avoid damaging him, making all possible tests, scanning and screening him to see whether anything has gone awry. By viewing the possible future child, while he is still a hypothetical nothing, as if he were already a patient needing all these precautions—and only so—can we bring ourselves to believe that minimizing the risks is enough. That *is* enough for an ordinary patient in the bush, but not enough for a patient in the hand, i.e., literally, "manipulated," in vitro, before he ever was. But to manipulate a patient into being requires at least the far more stringent requirement that to do this we must know that every possibility of damage from the procedure itself has surely been foreclosed. That stipulation the manipulation of embryos is not likely to meet. Anyone familiar with discussions of the moral limits upon human experimentation would say, I think, that the stipulation cannot be met. Medicine must certainly violate it before learning how to meet it, even if the first implanted baby turns out to be a Mahalia Jackson and not a monstrosity or mentally retarded. An experiment must be moral in its inception, as Dr. Henry K. Beecher said so often—it does not become moral because it happens to produce good results.

Since medicine manipulates human beings—sometimes at great risk, always at some risk—in order to persuade ourselves that we are permitted to manipulate a baby into being, at some risk, the unmade baby must be vaguely thought of as somehow already in being. So Dr. Edwards, in a scientific (not a popular) presentation of the state of the art, revealingly referred to one of his patients as "the mother."[9]

Whether physicians engaged in this practice in fact vaguely think in this way or not, they must act as if the baby already has being in order to think it sufficient simply to do everything thereafter to minimize the risks. By the ordinary canons of medical ethics, the unmade child has not "volunteered" to help the scientist—or even his "mother." If the possible future human being can be construed to have "volunteered," we would have first to construe him to be there, in being, or at least with a powerful title to be born, willing to suffer some induced risk in order to be manipulated to "come unto us." To construe his consent requires not only these manifest absurdities; to do so, to consent in his behalf, would also require that he be already exposed to some risk which these procedures are designed to relieve. For, again by the ordinary canons of medical ethics, we are not permitted to give proxy consent except medically in behalf of someone who may not be in a position to give expressed consent, or to impute to him a will to relieve someone else's condition—in his case "his" "mother's" infertility. We ought not to choose for another the hazards he must bear, while choosing at the same time to give him life in which to bear them and to suffer our chosen experimentations. The putative volition of such an unmade child must, anyway, be said to be negative, since researchers who work in human experimentation do not claim that they are allowed to ask volunteers to face possibly suicidal risks or to place themselves at risk of serious deformity.

Before we conclude this part of an article to be continued in the next issue, it is worth calling attention to the fact that a negative moral verdict against in vitro fertilization need invoke no other standards of judgment than *the received principles of medical ethics.* I have appealed to no religious and to no other ethical criteria. Either the accepted principles of medical ethics must give way, or fabricated babies should not be ventured. In the next issue I shall offer additional reasons for never using technological "reproduction" to supplant human procreation.

Notes

1. Grossman E: The obsolescent mother: A scenario. *Altantic* 227:39–50 (May) 1971. *Medical World News* (April 4, 1969, p. 27) quotes Dr. Edwards' statement in full: "We tell the women with blocked oviducts, 'Your only hope of having a child is to help us. Then maybe we can help you.' " The question is whether the single word "maybe" communicates the fact that the physicians likely did not *mean* actually to attempt to overcome childlessness in most, if any, of the cases so far. The statement that artificial fertilization is the woman's "only hope" was simply false—unless there were *medical* reasons why none of these women were patients on whom oviduct reconstruction (see below) or superovulation might have been tried. (In one series of 46 women, three promptly became pregnant as a result of the superovulatory drug administered as a part of the procedure to collect oocytes.) And, of course, if "hope" is a proper subject for medical treatment, adoption was also an alternative.

   The question of defective consent arises in another form in the case of experiments in the 1950s performed by Dr. Landrum Shettles of Columbia University's College of Physicians and Surgeons. He was *not* trying to overcome the barrier of oviduct trouble to enable his "patients" to have a baby. Instead, as one recent account puts it: "In the course of performing various operations requiring abdominal incision into the peritoneal cavity of the female, Dr. Shettles pierced the ovaries of his patients with a syringe and aspirated . . . some of the eggs from their follicles . . . without harming the patient in any way. . . ." (Rorvik, D. M.: The test-tube baby is coming. *Look* May 18, 1971, p. 83). The question is not whether Dr. Shettles *harmed* these patients in any way, but whether they *consented* in any way to have a procedure done to them that was wholly unrelated to the condition that called for the abdominal incision to be made.

2. Grossman, E., *op. cit.*; also Rorvik, D. M., *op. cit.*, p. 85. Rorvik also describes Dr. Shettles as one among many "daring" experimenters who have "propelled mankind forward," and as *pressing on* in the face of criticism. This may be courage in the face of a scientist's "adversities." The question is whether this personal and professional "daring" has excluded or can exclude any possible damage to that possible future human being, before the scientist "dares" go ahead. If not, use of words like "bravery" or "courage" represents a serious degradation of our moral language.

   In a scientific article published as late in the course of these advances in experimental embryology as 1970, Dr. Edwards and colleagues stated flatly that "the normality of embryonic development and the efficiency of embryo transfer *cannot* yet be assessed" [italics added]. (Edwards, R. G., Steptoe, P. C., Purdy, J. M.: Fertilization and cleavage in vitro of preovulator human oocytes. *Nature* 227:1307–1309, 1970.) That cautionary statement from the scientists is related not only to the quality of courage discussed above; on this, the question will be whether these limits can ever be overcome without actions that are irremediably rash in dealing with viable progeny. The 1970 statement is also decisive in answering the question whether all the women who to date have been experimental subjects were deceived. They were, if no more was told them than "maybe we can help you."

3. Before desisting, Petrucci said he had maintained another fetus, a female, alive for a full 49 days before it died owing to a "technical mistake." In 1966 the Russian scientists announced they had kept 250 fetuses alive beyond the record Petrucci claimed; one lived, they said, for six months and weighed 510 gm (1 lb 2 oz) before dying. (Francoeur, R. T.: *Utopian Motherhood.* Garden City, N.Y., Doubleday & Co., Inc., 1970, p. 58.)
4. Francoeur, R. T., ibid, pp. 59–60.
5. Greet, K., quoted in Francoeur, R. T., ibid, p. 74.
6. Cohn, V.: Lab growth of human embryo raises doubt of "normality." *Washington Post* March 21, 1971.
7. Six years ago Dr. Edwards was also more cautious; indeed, he seemed to believe culturing eggs for the treatment of human infertility faced insurmountable practical and moral objections. "If rabbit and pig eggs grown in culture can be fertilized after maturation in culture, presumably human eggs grown

in culture could also be fertilized, *although obviously it would not be permissible to implant them in a human recipient.* We have therefore attempted to fertilize human eggs in vitro [italics added]." That is, in order to study the process of human fertilization and early growth, precisely *not* in order to produce a child-to-be. (Edwards, R. G.: Mammalian eggs in the laboratory. *Sci Amer* 215:73–81 [Aug] 1966.)

8. Harris, M. (ed.): *Early Diagnosis of Human Genetic Defects: Scientific and Ethical Considerations*, Symposium jointly sponsored by the John E. Fogarty International Center for Advanced Study in the Health Sciences, National Institutes of Health, Bethesda, Md., May 18–19, 1970, U.S. Government Printing Office, 1972, p. 182.
9. Edwards, R. G., Steptoe, P. C., Purdy, J. M., op. cit. pp. 1307–1309. If these women were patients for infertility, Leon Kass remarks (Hamilton, M. [ed.]: *Three Medical Futures.* Grand Rapids, Mich., Wm. B. Eerdmans Publishing Co., 1972), then "mothers" is surely the one thing they are not.

II. Rejoinders and Future Forecast

IN THE PREVIOUS issue of THE JOURNAL[1] I set forth the ethical objections against in vitro fertilization and embryo transplantation which can be drawn from applying to these experiments the received standards of medical ethics. Unless the ethics of the medical research profession is to be radically revised or abandoned, we ought not to manipulate at risk the child-to-be. I now want to take up certain answers to my argument. From the nature of these rejoinders we can clearly see the extent to which human procreation has already been replaced by the idea of "manufacturing" our progeny. Unless and until *that* concept is reversed, mankind's movement toward Aldous Huxley's Hatcheries must surely prove irreversible.

It may be granted that the mimicry of natural fertilization, implantation, and the environment of the womb cannot be guaranteed to be perfect or without possibly harmful, induced impairments to the possible future child. It may be granted that the last possible testing procedure may itself have induced damage, or the last one—necessarily omitted (because it might damage)—could mean a *failure* to detect damage previously induced. It may be granted that subsequent screening procedures by amniocentesis or scanning by fetoscopy (when this is developed) themselves may not catch every possible earlier mishap and that these procedures (which are only "distant" inspections in comparison with embryo manipulation) may themselves do some damage to the unborn child. In short, the facts on which my foregoing argument is based may be granted.

But then it will be said that there are advantages that can be gained for the possible future human being. While scanning for procedurally induced damage and doing everything possible to reduce any remaining incidence of mishap, we can detect naturally inborn metabolic "error" or chromosomal disorder and eliminate these before human life comes to term. Even if natural fertilization and the uterine environment have been selected over long evolutionary ages, still there are "mistakes" in nature and the uterine environment turns out to be harsh to many. The incidence of these "natural" damages is not negligible, and the incidence of possible induced damage can be kept within acceptable bounds, it can be argued, so that the balance of added induced risks and subtracted natural risks can be (by screening, followed by abortion) to the comparative benefit of the possible future human being created by embryo implantation.

If this is said—and to be sure, it will always be said—the rebuttals are two. First, at its face value, that is no argument at all against the previously stated reasons for prohibiting in vitro fertilization and embryo transplantation. The alleged compensating advantage—the avoidance of a life of suffering from inborn errors, chromosomal disorders, or other "natural" damage—is no advantage to the individual we are talking about, because he would not have been subject to those very risks (plus the additional risks) had he not been *artificially* conceived. The rejoinder assumes his conception, and that was the issue under discussion. To obtain the avoidance of the evils which are here said to counterbalance a minimum incidence of induced risks, one has to presuppose the unconceived child has overriding title to be born, or his mother an absolute right to have a child, or that he somehow is already in the land of the living so that we should go to work on him preconceptually, applying the usual balancing medical judgments that are applicable to existing patients. Rather than rehearse that scenario, let me say simply that no one can cause an ethical conclusion justifying in vitro fertilization to bottom on its own premise, nor can he warrant doing that procedure by appeals which in mente assume it has already taken place.

My second point is the more important one. This rejoinder

to my argument itself shows clearly that anyone who offers it or is persuaded by it has already in mente placed artificial fertilization and gestation on a parity with the natural processes of human procreation. He has already incipiently stated the conditions under which manufacturing *should* replace human reproduction entirely. The quality of the "product" is the overriding issue; one comparable damage is interchangeable with another whether done by men or accepted by them; one incidence of risk cancels another like incidence, whether the one or the other comes from nature or from the biological laboratory.

This is important to note here because a most important societal reason for opposing in vitro fertilization is what is called the "thin edge of the wedge" argument, the "camel's nose under the tent" argument. This is a good argument if one is concerned at all about wisdom in the practice of medicine, in public policy, or in received social outlooks. To be valid, however, the wedge argument need not, like my reasons drawn from medical ethics, attempt to show the inherent immorality of a given sort of action or practice. It need only show that if we do this particular action or permit or encourage a particular practice (perhaps because of undeniable immediate values, e.g., enabling a woman to have a child), we will influence others and cause ourselves to take following steps that in foreseeable succession add up to immense disvalue for the human community. So we shall have to assess in vitro fertilization as a long step toward Hatcheries, i.e., extracorporeal gestation, and the introduction of unlimited genetic changes into human germinal material while it is being cultured by the Conditioners and Predestinators of the future.

The truth is, however, that the reasons the wedge argument "works" are not solely extrinsic, not solely because narrow concentration on present values causes us to forget deleterious effects on future values, not solely because we may incline ourselves and others to do things we cannot later avoid because we have lost the capacity to wish otherwise. Instead, the wedge argument "works," chiefly though not exclusively, because incipiently and intrinsically the reasoning behind the justification of a present practice already *in principle* embraces those other societal practices as well. This intrinsic connection does not compel us to take those other steps also, but the argument for so doing has already impressed itself on our minds and persuaded us in the case at hand. We will have to pull the laboring oar against our present reasons if we are not to proceed further along the line already taken.

This, I believe, is clearly the case in regard to in vitro fertilization and embryo implantation. Ostensibly, the end in view is therapeutic, the altogether praiseworthy objective of enabling a woman to have a child of her own. But when objection is raised that this should not be done *by these means*, which cannot be guaranteed not to be injurious to the child, the only possible answer is and logically must be that those who justify this procedure mean in all sorts of other ways to control and predetermine the "product." This means that in mente and in principle, human procreation has already been interchanged with manufacture, if, as, and when we can calculate that we can do so at lesser costs to the "product" than nature affords. Since under the surface this is the essence of the steps now taken, all the rest need be only technical accomplishments. When they follow it will not be because of extrinsic influences (which the wedge argument summarizes) but because our reasons here and now went wrong.

For example, apart from the needed balancing judgments about the qualifications of the product of in vitro fertilization and embryo implantation, what are we to say about the claim that this "therapy" is only devoted to curing a woman's infertility? Doctors Edwards and Sharpe[2] say that "while the physical health of the parents does not demand that their infertility be cured," still "infertility seems to be a clinical defect to be remedied if possible by medical attention." Is the "clinical defect" of infertility remedied by in vitro fertilization? I should say not! Instead, the child as a product of technology is to be brought forth, without remedying the woman's infertility. She remains as infertile as before. No wonder, then, that the chief concern about the child is whether as a product more damage from his natural genesis may be removed than may be caused by producing him in this way. If infertility is a "clinical defect" which should be remedied, that would seem to call for reconstructive surgery on the oviducts, from which 30% to 50% success has been reported. Therapy is applied directly to the defect needing remedy. The woman is made fertile, and she in her marriage transmits life to her child.

By contrast in vitro fertilization is arguably *not* a *medical* procedure. It concentrates on the "product," not on a medical condition which itself can be cured, if at all, only in the only actual patient there is. Instead, without curing that condition, in vitro fertilization concentrates on a product; it is therefore manufacture by biological technology, not medicine.[3] To construe this procedure as a practice of medicine, we have to construe medicine to be devoted to the satisfaction of desires.

Edwards and Sharpe say,[4] "the desire to have children must be among the most basic human instincts, and denying it can lead to considerable psychological and social difficulties." Alas, and of course! Still our question remains. If medicine enables a couple to have a child by means other than endeavors to correct the woman's infertility itself, if medicine undertakes to produce the result without curing the defect, if medicine turns to doctoring *desires* instead of medical conditions, if medicine provides a woman with a child without actually curing her infertility, is there any reason for doctors to be reluctant to accede to parents' desire to have a girl rather than a boy, blond hair rather than brown, a genius rather than a clout, a Horowitz in the family rather than a tone-deaf child, or alternatively a child who because of his idiosyncracies would have a good career as a freak in the circus?

"The procedures leading to replacement and implantation *open the way* to further work on human embryos in the laboratory," [italics added] state Edwards and Sharpe.[5] In addition to the benign work of preventing the birth of children with genetic defects to which the way is open, these authors also mention cloning, and the creation of "chimeras" by adding to an embryo the precursor cells for organs from other blastocysts (perhaps from other species). For these authors, "the beginning of medical ethics . . . *primum non nocere*" permits alleviation of infertility. They note that this "*has been stretched* to cover destruction of foetuses with hereditary defects" [italics added]. Then they ask: could medical ethics be "stretched" to justify "the more remote techniques like modifying embryos?"—chimeras?[6] I suggest that the answer to that question is plainly, Yes. Not because the principles of medical ethics can be stretched so far, but because they have been *replaced* by the principles, if any, governing biological manufacture. This radical displacement happens long before we begin adding to possible future human beings organs not their own. It happens rather when we employ medical technology to "alleviate infertility" by producing the result without treating any medical condition and without alleviating any medical defect.

The point I want to make is simply that there is a correlation (which benevolent motives do not excuse) between the devotion of medical science to manufacturing the child as a "product" or to altering the child into varying products and the devotion of medical science to the treatment of human *desires* (be these desires sound, whimsical, or demonic). The important line lies between doctoring desires (which are bound to be ingenious) and seeking to correct a medical condition if it is possible to do so. Across this line, medical science has made a step—and might as well and will go further—in attempting to produce a baby without first actually curing a woman's infertility. After all, who is to say that having another wrong-gendered child is not as unacceptable a result to some parents as not having a child at all? If medical practice has an obligation to guarantee one of these wishes, it may have an obligation to guarantee the other, and many more besides. In my opinion, medical practice loses its way into an entirely different human activity—manufacture (which most wants to satisfy desires)—if it undertakes either to produce a child without curing infertility as a condition or to produce simply the desired sort of child.

Elsewhere I have pointed out[7] that a significant move toward in vitro fertilization and all the rest was made when first we began to use a manufacturing term—"reproduction"—for procreation, human parenthood, and transmission of life through life by the generating generations of mankind. Scientists working in the field of "reproductive biology" have now drawn not improper conclusions from the linguistic mistake. It is indeed possible for experimental embryologists to "conceive" of alternative modes of "reproduction"—if that, strictly, is what we mean by conception and parenthood.

What is at stake in avoiding every action or thought suggestive of manufacturing whenever we speak of parenthood has been well expressed by Dr. Leon Kass, executive secretary of the Committee on the Life Sciences and Social Policy, National Academy of Sciences. I cannot improve upon his reflections on this subject:

Human procreation is human partly because it is not simply an activity of our rational wills. Men and women are embodied as well as desiring and calculating creatures. It is for the gods to create in thought and by fiat (Let the earth bring forth . . .). And some future race of demigods (or demi-men) may obtain its survivors from the local fertilization and decanting station. But *human* procreation is begetting. It is a more complete human activity precisely because it engages us bodily and spiritually, as well as rationally. Is there possibly some wisdom in that mystery of nature which joins the pleasure of sex, the communication of love and the desire for children in the very activity by which we continue the chain of human existence? Is biological parenthood a built-in device selected to promote the adequate caring for children? Before embarking on New Beginnings in Life we should consider the meaning of the union between sex, love and procreation, and the meaning and consequence of its cleavage.

What is new is nothing more radical than the divorce of the generation of new life from human sexuality and ultimately from the confines of the human body, a separation which began with artificial insemination and which will finish with ectogenesis, the full laboratory growth of a baby from sperm to term. What is new is that sexual intercourse will no longer be needed for generating new life. This piece of novelty leads to two others: there is a new co-progenitor (or several such), the embryologist-geneticist-physican, and there is a new home for generation, the laboratory. The mysterious and intimate processes of generation are to be moved from the darkness of the womb to the bright (fluorescent) light of the laboratory, and beyond the shadow of a single doubt.

The Hebrews, impressed with the phenomenon of transmitting life from father to son, used a word we translate "begetting" or "siring." The Greeks, impressed with the springing forth of new life in the cyclical processes of generation and decay, called it genesis, from a root meaning "to come into being." (It was the Greek translators who gave this name to the first book of the Hebrew Bible.) The pre-modern Christian English-speaking world, impressed with the world as given by a Creator, used the term pro-creation. We, impressed with the machine and the gross national product, our own work of creation, employ a metaphor of the factory, re-production. And Aldous Huxley has provided "decantation" for that technology-worshipping Brave New World of to-morrow.[8]

In conclusion, I now turn to the "wedge argument" and the final triumph of manufacturing over human parent-hood. "Decantation" has been in our future for some time now—at least from the time we began seriously to think of children as the means by which we "reproduce."

In a 1951 pronouncement against artificial insemination as

a mode of transmitting human life, Pope Pius XII said that "to reduce the cohabitation of married persons and the conjugal act to a mere organic function for the transmission of the germ of life would be to convert the domestic hearth, sanctuary of the family, into nothing more than a biological laboratory."[9] Now, since I am not a Roman Catholic, I do not believe that in that statement the Holy Father told me anything I might not have known anyway. That's different from saying that had the Pope in fact not said it, I would have had occasion actually to discern the signs of the times with wisdom enough to see the significance of the first major step taken in the twentieth century which eventually will replace human procreation with laboratory manufacture. The fact is that in 1951 the Pope communicated nothing to me by that statement; I've looked it up since.

Still his warning is worthy of reexamination today as we face yet more steps—all leading with accelerated rapidity toward the same end.

The memory of the Holy See—as Lord Macaulay pointed out in the last century—is very long, much longer than any other political or social body in the modern world. It is not easy to judge whether from the eminence of the Vatican and its long institutional memory there accrues to the Pontiff a prescience to see the deeper deleterious trends in present events which lesser mortals always appraise and approve in terms of their seeming immediate benefits. Still, it is worth pondering whether this may be the case or not, since teams of scientists are now hard at work assaulting the entire process of human gestation—the beginning, the middle, and the end—and, now that technical possibilities and "liberal" abortion attitudes have given them free access to the uterus, they are threatening to move life's beginnings from sperm to term entirely into the laboratory. (And we can ask of that, what would the terminus be?) These developments seem likely in historical perspective to render Pius XII's 1951 statement one of the earliest and wisest warnings to humankind to be spoken by someone having some degree of moral and spiritual authority; and a call to heed the warnings of other prophetic insights and voices that are ever more muted or forgotten as our modern world, defendable step by defendable step, moves ineluctably toward the state of affairs these wise men discerned with almost unbearable dread and foreboding.

Two of these are worth mention. In 1932 Aldous Huxley published *Brave New World*, with its principal mechanisms, the pharmacological management of contentment and the Fertilizing and Decanting Rooms in the East London Hatchery. In 1947, C. S. Lewis published a book bearing the title *The Abolition of Man*. Lewis submitted man's project of gaining ever increasing power over nature to merciless analysis; his message rings as clear and true as a bell on a Sabbath morning in early New England (if anyone wants to revisit either). Since Lewis' book is less well known than Huxley's, its burden can briefly be set forth by means of the following quotations:[10]

> What we call Man's power over Nature turns out to be a power exercised by some men over other men with Nature as its instrument. . . . And all long-term exercises of power, especially in breeding, must mean the power of earlier generations over later ones. . . . If any age really attains, by eugenics and scientific education, the power to make its descendants what it pleases, all men who live after it are the patients of that power. . . . And if, as is almost certain, the age which has thus attained maximum power over posterity were also the age most emancipated from tradition, it would be engaged in reducing the power of its predecessors almost as drastically as that of its successors. . . . The last men, far from being the heirs of power will be of all men most subject to the dead hand of the great planners and conditioners and will themselves exercise least power upon the future. . . . There neither is nor can be any simple increase of power on Man's side. Each new power won *by* man is a power *over* man as well. Each advance leaves him weaker as well as stronger. In every victory, besides being the general who triumphs, he is also the prisoner who follows the triumphal car. . . . The man-moulders of the new age . . .: we shall get at least a race of

> conditioners who really can cut all posterity in what shape they please. . . . Nature will be troubled no more by the restive species that rose in revolt against her so many millions of years ago, will be vexed no longer by its chatter of truth and mercy and beauty and happiness. *Ferum victorem capit:* and if the eugenics are efficient enough there will be no second revolt, but all snug beneath the Conditioners, and the Conditioners beneath her, till the moon falls or the sun grows cold. . . . [We should] not do to minerals and vegetables what modern science threatens to do to man himself.

Aldous Huxley and C. S. Lewis lived and wrote during the Hitler era, soon after World War II and at the beginning of the nuclear age. It is a striking and significant fact that they did not see the abuse of political power or nuclear destruction to be the greatest threats to the humanity of man. Lesser critics did. Instead, Lewis' analysis and Huxley's bitter social satire signaled out genetics, pharmacology, and experimental embryology as sources of the coming great evils. Pope Pius XII belongs at least among the minor prophets for condemning, in 1951, artificial insemination (if this was his meaning[11]) as a "defendable" step (defendable only in terms of one set of immediate values, but not in a larger view) along the way toward the transformation of human procreation into manufacture in biological laboratories (and therefore undefendable).

Because of the mounting possibilities of present and future biomedical interventions and embryo manipulations, one sees frequent references to Aldous Huxley, not only by science writers in popular periodicals but also in the medical and scientific literature. Almost always it is pointed out[12] how inaccurate Huxley was in the span of time he allowed for these powers to be in the grasp of man and practically applied. *Brave New World* begins on a day in 632 AF (After Ford!). That is, about six hundred years in the future. "Let us suppose the hundredth century AD," wrote C. S. Lewis[13] when he, too, imagined the achievement of mastery over the species. Most present-day references to Aldous Huxley in the scientific literature and in the popular press forget the social criticism, the biting satire; the authors seem happy if not triumphant in fastening upon the small point that Huxley was wrong in his calendar date. It is as if the author of *A Modest Proposal* (for increasing the food supply of Ireland by having the population eat their own children) were to be mildly chided for thinking it would take some time for his proposal to be adopted!

Forgotten also is the fact that *Brave New World* depicts a frictionless society made up of entirely happy people; indeed, in essential respects a *just* society measured by the standard of proportionate justice ("to equals, the equal; to unequals, the unequal"). Evidently Huxley saw quite clearly that there can be a grossly inhumane condition of mankind characterized by the greatest happiness altogether. This needs to be noted as we consider further steps along the way Huxley foresaw, viz., the embryo transplants to be done in the next few years. It is to be expected that this sort of manipulation of embryos can be justified in terms of our present perceptions of immediate happiness. Men will not suddenly enter *Brave New World* and be happy over such institutions as the Central Hatchery and Conditioning Center without a good deal of conditioning along the way. This will be called a "demand that social attitudes are *helped to keep pace* with" the increasing tempo of scientific advancement; the right of scientists to "exercise their professional activities *to the limit that is tolerable by society*," accepting some perhaps conservative collaboration "as *lay attitudes struggle to catch up with what the scientists can do*" [italics added].[14] Even now we can begin to learn to be happy with decantation instead of natural gestation, by stifling any moral doubts about in vitro fertilization and implantation of embryos. We should not be surprised if the value most concentrated on by most people is how happy the technique might make some people. At least, if Huxley was right in describing *Brave New World* as a happy place, we ought not to be surprised to find the way there to be a direction we are increasingly happy to take, our consciences formed exclusively by our biotechnical, pharmacological civilization as the impersonal Predestinator of our values.

The road to hell, they say, is paved with good intentions—to treat people's desires and their happiness. Thus, in reporting the plan to open commercial frozen sperm banks in New York City, *The New York Times*[15] said, in the second paragraph of the report, "That day is here now, not just as a laboratory curiosity but as a commercially available sperm banking service *that brings much closer the prospect of controlled breeding programs to produce superior members of the human species*" [italics added]. That prospect was prominently featured, not the short-range "defendable" "therapeutic" value, namely, that 85% of the clients of two sperm banks in other cities are men who have voluntarily undergone vasectomy. The name of one of the commercial firms also invoked other future possible uses, not the backstop provided by the sperm banks to men's willingness to use vasetomy for contraceptive purposes. This, too, is a part of the preconditioning by which we in the present age are persuading ourselves to be happy with Hatcheries; only the name for the institution in our future may be "Genetic Laboratories, Inc." It is clear that Huxley discerned something that (without a sea-change of values) is self-fulfilling in our culture; that indeed is the meaning of prophecy and prescience. It entails that generally we now are inclined to be persuaded of the immediate values of each step along the way to the final replacement of human procreation by laboratory manufacture. Otherwise, *Brave New World* would not be the happy place it will be. Conversely, if we could not be conditioned to contentment, there would be alarms now; and a wrenching away from the strange notion that every opposing moral attitude is always retrograde and should be repressed as we "struggle to catch up with what the scientists can do."

Mr. C. S. Lewis, as we noticed, said that we should "not do to minerals and vegetables what modern science threatens to do to man himself."[16] That statement, connecting as it does with contemporary ecological awareness, may be viewed by people today as a further evidence of Lewis' remarkable prescience. The point, however, is that Lewis discerned that the last citadel from which technological applications are apt to be excluded or where we will discover limits we will agree to defend as we would defend our lives is the citadel of man's nature itself. The wounds we have inflicted upon natural objects for lack of a proper sense of the natural environment are becoming clear to us—the lashes and the ecological backlash. Today many are testifying to the spiritual autonomy of all natural objects and to arrogance over none; to the scheme of things in which man has his place. But there is as yet no discernible evidence that we are recovering a sense for man as a natural object, too, toward whom a like form of "natural piety" is appropriate.

While the leopard, the great whale, and the forests are to be protected by restoring in mankind a proper sense of things, man as a natural being is to be given no such protection. There are aspects of the cheetah's existence that ought not to be violated, but none of man's. Other species are to be protected in their natural habitat and in their natural functions, but man is not.

Today the statement of Aristotle is amply verified: it would indeed be odd if a flute-player or artisan of any kind, a carpenter or a cobbler—or the mountain goat and the falcon—"have certain works and courses of action," while "Man as Man has none, but is left by Nature without a work" of his own.[17] It may be that Aristotle's question, What is the work of man? is expressed in language that will seem too functional for the ecological ethics we need in locating man in the creation of which we are a part and toward which we should have a "natural piety." Still, his view that all things in nature "have certain works and courses of action" has enough amplitude to be helpful as we search for a sense of man as a natural object too. Procreation, parenthood, is certainly one of those "courses of action" natural to man, which cannot without violation be disassembled and put together again—any more than we have the wisdom or the right impiously to destroy the environment of which we are a part rather than working according to its lineaments, according to the functions we discover to be the case in the whole assemblage of natural objects.

If St. Francis preached to his sisters the birds, spoke of his brother fire, called the turtle doves his little sisters, and composed a canticle to his brother the sun (and for this has been proposed as the patron saint of all ecologists), what are we to say of our brother man and of ourselves? If the commandment to "subdue the earth" is a right devilish one or else sorely in need of a loose, or of another, interpretation—an interpretation properly limited by man's vocation to tend the garden of God's creation—are we then to say that man is let loose here with the proper task of disassembling his own "courses of action," making himself and his own species wholly plastic to ingenious scientific interventions and alterations?

So today we have the oddity that men are preparing to play God over the human species while many among us are denying themselves that role over other species in nature. There is a renewed sense of the sacredness of groves, of the fact that air and streams should not be violated. At the same time, there is no abatement of acceptance of the view that human parenthood can be taken apart and reassembled in Oxford, England, New York, and Washington, D.C.; and, of course, it follows that thereafter human nature has to be wrought by Predestinators in the Decanting and Conditioning Rooms of the East London Hatchery and in commercial firms bearing the name "Genetic Laboratories, Inc." in all our metropolitan centers.

I have no explanation of why there is not among medical scientists an upsurge of protest against turning the profession of medical care into a technological function; why there is not, precisely today, a strong renewal of the view that the proper objective of medicine is to serve and care for man as a natural object, to help in all our natural "courses of action," to tend the garden of our creation. (Of the two oldest helping professions, the priesthood has long since abandoned magic to bring about extraordinary interruptions of natural processes; today, the mantle of such priestly incantations seems to have fallen on a core of medical researchers.)

Still there seems to be an evident, simple explanation of why people generally in all the advanced industrial countries of the world are apt to raise no serious objection, or apt at least to yield, to what the manipulation of embryos will surely do to ourselves and our progeny. It is a final irony to realize why invasions will now be done on man that we are slowly learning not to do on other natural objects; why natural human "courses of action" will be disassembled in an age in which we have learned to deplore strip mining; why in actual practice minerals and vegetables may be more respected than human parenthood, and mankind be ushered happily into *Brave New World.*

The reason will be not only that the agents of these vast changes are authority figures in white coats promising the benefits of applied knowledge. That, in other areas, we have learned to doubt in some degree. The deeper reason is that the agents of these vast changes, defendable step by defendable step, are deemed by the public to be not researchers mainly, but members of the healing profession, those who care for us, who tend the human condition.[18] Before it is realized that the objective has ceased to be the treatment of a *medical* condition, it will be too late; and Huxley will have been proved true. The people of a biomedical technical civilization, like the blind, aged Isaac, are apt to give their blessing to Jacob because of his venison and because his arms are smooth and hairy (with the skin of animals), while the voice and the future will not be those of Esau or anyone's first born (Genesis 27:19–29).

Dr. Joshua Lederberg, speaking of how public policy may be determined in regard to clonal reproduction, ventured the opinion that this would depend on "the accident of the first advertised examples . . . the batting average, or public esteem of the clonant; the handsomeness of the para-human product. . . ."[19] If Aldous Huxley had any insight into our times, perhaps one can express the paradoxical and macabre "hope" that the first example of the production of a child by in vitro fertilization and embryo transplant will prove to be a bad result—and that it will be well advertised, not hidden from view! I do not actually believe that the good to come from public revulsion in such an event would justify the impairment of that child. But then, for the same reasons, neither is the manipulation of embryos a procedure that can possibly be morally justified.

Notes

1. Ramsey, P.: Shall we "reproduce"? I. The medical ethics of in vitro fertilization. *JAMA* 220:1346–1350, 1972.
2. Edwards, R. G., Sharpe, D. J.: Social values and research in human embryology. *Nature* 231:87–91, 1971.
3. Anyone advancing this argument will promptly be subjected to a barrage of information he is supposed not to know about medicine's technological armamentarium. That is a very damaging defense: it reduces the baby to the status of a prosthesis for the permanent cure of his mother's condition.
4. Edwards, R. G., Sharpe, D. J., *op. cit.*, p. 87.
5. *Ibid.*, p. 87.
6. *Ibid.*, p. 89.
7. Ramsey, P.: *Fabricated Man: The Ethics of Genetic Control.* New Haven, Conn., Yale University Press, 1970, p. 137.
8. Kass, L. R.: New beginnings in life, in Hamilton, M. (ed.): *The New Genetics and the Future of Man.* Grand Rapids, Mich., Wm. B. Eerdmans Co., 1972, pp. 14–63; also: Making babies: The new biology and the "old" morality. *Public Interest*, No. 26, 1972, pp. 19–56.
9. *Acta Apostolicae Sedis*, 43:850, 1951.
10. Lewis, C. S.: *The Abolition of Man.* New York, Macmillan Co., 1947.
11. See Richard A. McCormick, S.J.: Notes on moral theology: April-September 1970. *Theological Studies* 32:95–97, 1971.
12. For example, Francoeur says that Huxley "tried to picture the world of *six hundred hence,* a world which is *already with us*" [italics added]. (Francoeur, R. T.: *Utopian Motherhood:*

New Trends in Human Reproduction. Garden City, N.Y., Doubleday & Co., Inc., 1970, p. 56.

13. Lewis, C. S., *op. cit.*, p. 37.
14. Edwards, R. G., Sharpe, D. J., *op. cit.*, pp. 87, 90. Even so, Dr. Bentley Glass, former president of the American Association for the Advancement of Science, regards the public utterances of Edwards and his colleagues as too cautious and conservative. "It should be obvious," Glass writes, "that the technique can be quickly and widely extended." (Glass, P.: Endless horizons or golden age? *Science* 171:23–29, 1971.)
15. Rensberger, B.: From the day of deposit: A lien on the future. *New York Times*, Aug. 22, 1971.
16. Lewis, C. S., *op. cit.*, p. 49.
17. Aristotle: *Nichomachean Ethics*, 1097b.
18. In addition to this account, there are additional specific reasons why spokesmen of Church and Synagogue, against all their former principles, are today especially vulnerable to futuristic blandishments.
19. Lederberg, J.: Experimental genetics and human evolution. *The American Naturalists* 100:519–531, 1966; reprinted, *Bulletin of the Atomic Scientists* 22:4–11, 1966.

Toward a Theology of Eugenics

William Vrasdonk

On the basis of his understanding of the evolutionary process, William Vrasdonk contends that theologians should not categorically oppose all forms of genetic engineering. Those theologians who warn against artificial changes in man's genetic structure do so on the basis of a misplaced understanding of the doctrine of original sin: "By creating his own future, man is not playing God; he is responding in faith and trust to the language of events addressing him." Nonetheless, man must not take inappropriate action; attentive to the integrity of the evolutionary process, he will "not change his environment indiscriminately." A native of the Netherlands, Dr. Vrasdonk teaches in the Department of Theological Studies at the University of Dayton, Ohio, where he has specialized in evolutionary ethics and the theology of hope. In March 1972 he organized a national interdisciplinary Conference on Immortality, at which scientists, futurists, philosophers, and theologians from different universities presented papers on the prospect of immortality. His article first appeared in the November-December 1971 issue of *The Ecumenist.**

PAUL TILLICH tried to interpret faith in contemporary terms. While it had been customary to regard a believer in God or a religious person as one who acknowledged God's existence and related himself to this God in trust, prayer, and thanksgiving, Tillich tried to show that faith, religious faith, may be a reality in persons who are no longer willing to talk about God. Faith is ultimate concern. Tillich recognized the religious quality of any person who

* 1865 Broadway, New York, N.Y. 10023.

seriously questions the meaning of existence as a whole and the importance of his own being within this totality. When man is ultimately concerned about something that is clearly a limited part of reality, then he is threatened by idolatry. But when his concern embraces the total reality, however this may be interpreted, then he is open to the divine. He is religious whether he talks about God or not.

When Tillich interpreted faith in this manner, he was a pioneer. Since that time a great number of theologians in the Protestant and Catholic Churches, while not following the exact thought of Tillich, have come to look upon faith as man's relationship to the deepest dimension of reality, spell out the meaning of faith in secular terms, and define faith in such a way that even a graced outsider may participate in it. Faith, Spirit-created faith, is "an abiding feature of man's mode of existence as a person" (Karl Rahner, "Faith," *Sacramentum Mundi*).

Faith and Evolution

While many theologians have come to interpret faith in this manner, they do not usually face all the consequences that follow from this interpretation. It has become necessary to abandon any idea of God as the heavenly Father, the Creator of the universe, who after finishing his creation rules the world according to his gracious providence. In the perspective adopted by contemporary theologians, God is present to the universe as Creator, creation is still ongoing, and his providence refers not to an eternal plan in the divine mind, but to the graciousness whereby he enables man to create his own future. To say that creation is ongoing, therefore, introduces the theologian inevitably to an evolutionary perspective; we have come to be where we are now through a slow development in which God was at work, and our future is still to be made by a divinely oriented process in which not only the cosmos, but we ourselves are involved.

Conversation with scientists and philosophers concerned about cosmic evolution has become important for the contemporary theologian. Among scientists the appreciation of evolution differs in quality. Darwin presented as a scientific conclusion that blind chance was a significant factor in biological evolution; his view, needless to say, does not leave any room for divine providence. Yet even if it is only luck that has made the life-process evolve, it is still an incomprehensible amount of good luck that is displayed in evolution. In other words, the observable progressive tendency of the evolutionary process suggests that there is an awe-inspiring amount of good will behind it. This tendency was so obvious to Julian Huxley that he made it his religion to believe in the progressive drift of the evolutionary process (cf. *Religion without Revelation*). Even when it is only by means of mutations—which are evaluated at times as errors in the transmission of the genetic information within the species—there exists the openness toward growth and development. Evolution actually takes place! The degree of this openness is amazing if we consider that more than a million years ago the human race did not exist. And now here we are. We populate the whole earth, and our intentions are directed to the universe—already man has walked on the moon.

If the goodness of the creative energy is thus observable and awe-inspiring to an atheistic, humanistic scholar like Julian Huxley, could not the goodness of the creative force be experienced by other sensitive, even if less learned people? After all, all forms of existence participate in the evolutionary drift. What is the energy by which life has emerged and what takes hold of existence in such multifarious ways? The dead-looking trees in the winter have already hidden within them the germ of new leaves and blossoms that will come to full splendor in the warmth of the springtime sun. Why did animals creep out of the water and start their amazing history of life-development on dry soil? Why did birds want to fly and why did other birds develop feathers of splendid colors? Why do people, men and women, reach out for each other and make love? Why is not tragedy more potent and more effective in diminishing the life forces? Why is it that many pessimists still hang on to life? Why is there a certain order in the universe? These questions have been answered in many ways. But more important than the rational answer is man's experience of the creative goodness and his openness to it. This sort of religious experience is found everywhere, even when it is not discerned as such.

There are many people who feel that the goodness operative in the evolution of the universe and development of life is in some way also operative in themselves as source of energy and direction of growth. How is this religious openness related to the biblical faith?

God Speaks in the Cosmos

Some theologians wish to make a radical distinction between the trusting openness to the evolutionary summons and the biblical faith. In his *Evolutionary Philosophies and Contemporary Theology*, Eric C. Rust examines and evaluates the various process theologies formulated by such thinkers as Hegel, Teilhard de Chardin, Whitehead, Hartshorne, Cobb, Bergson, and Temple. While Rust shows an appreciation for process thought and praises the various authors for their serious regard of history and the evolutionary drive encountered in all forms of existence, he does not think that these thinkers do justice to the biblical message. God in these theories is not personal; he is not the God of grace, freedom and mercy. God is here fitted into elaborate theories; his personal uniqueness is depersonalized and determined by the rationale of a universal system.

Is this the only Christian conclusion? Surely not. Theologians are divided on this issue. For many contemporary theologians the easy objectification and personalization of

God as Creator of the universe and Father of mankind introduces a practical dualism into life that is hard to harmonize with the thrust of the Christian message today. If the universe is simply God's handiwork, then it is not the real thing; then only he is the really real. This leads to a trivialization of history and an insincere participation in the creative process of the universe. Here God's ongoing creation, his very presence to human life and the cosmos, is not recognized.

It was because of such a dualism that Julian Huxley rejected the existence of a personal God. A personal God, Huxley thought, would inevitably distract people from the really real—the evolutionary process. The British scientist recognized in nature a dimension that commands awe and amazement, the "stuff of divinity," which is the religious and transcendental "raw material" out of which men have fashioned their divinities (cf. "The New Divinity," *Essays of a Humanist*). The intentionality of this famous atheist is directed toward the promotion of an all-out sincerity for participating in the processes of the universe.

The same kind of sincerity is promoted by some theologians. Martin Buber finds strong formulations to give expression to this ultimate concern. He regards it as foolish to seek God in a way of separation, in any form of piety or liturgy that is not a means for intensifying man's quest for life itself. It is Buber's conviction that the exploration of life with openness will lead to the unfathomable. It is there, in a sensitive and intelligent dedication to life itself, that man encounters the living God. We are continually addressed by events. It is in this "language of events" that the divine Word speaks to us.

The theologian must study whether Huxley's "stuff of divinity" and Buber's "language of events" refer to the same religious aspect of the life-creating process. They seem to refer to something that went on prior to man's own entry into history. Open and positive response to the inviting possibilities of the evolutionary process, or the listening to the language of events, occurred long before the human race emerged on this earth. Humanity itself is the product of the faithful openness and religious response of all the ancestors of the first man. Religion in the sense of openness and commitment was already present in atom, chemicals, and cells as well as in higher animals insofar as they showed the willingness to cooperate in the evolutionary production of mankind. They responded to the language of events.

Whether theologians take seriously the evolutionary process as the locus of God's creative presence to life is not a purely theoretical issue. It has significant practical consequences. It affects, for instance, the theological approach to eugenics.

The Improvement of Man's Genetic Structure

Well-known theologians (Paul Ramsey, Charles Curran, and Helmut Thielicke) have warned Christians against all forms of genetic engineering to change and improve man's capacities. Instead of basing themselves on a theological understanding of evolution and the language of events, they refer mainly to man's sinfulness. "Don't touch," they say. Born in the inherited sin and inevitably affected by it, man is always tempted to interfere in the divine order of creation and spoil it. Worse than that, man is tempted to play God and arrogate to himself a presumptuous lordship over the universe. These theologians invoke these two tendencies of sinful man to warn modern scientists not to get involved in genetic engineering. Don't touch the genetic structure of man; if you do, you will make this structure worse and, in addition to this, your own act of pride will destroy you.

The question whether or not to go ahead with genetic engineering and to make artificial changes in the genetic structure of mankind is indeed a complex and difficult problem. Geneticists are well aware of this. But theologians do not make a useful contribution to the conversation with geneticists if they refuse to reflect on man's and the universe's religious openness to the evolutionary process. In this context, the reference to original sin is misplaced.

In contemporary studies on the sinfulness of the human condition, man's sin tends to be equated with his pathological resistance to growth and development. Sin is man's resistance to grace. If man is situated in an environment in which God summons him to move, to grow, to expand, and to transform the world as well as himself, then man's sin must be seen primarily in his defenses, his passivity, his unwillingness to respond, and his compulsive repetitions of an earlier stage of his life. Man is divinely summoned, these theologians show, to assume responsibility for himself and his world. Man's sin lies not in the courageous response to this summons, but precisely in his fearful refusal to assume the responsibility for the future. By creating his own future, man is not playing God; he is responding in faith and trust to the language of events addressing him.

In the symbolic language of Christian doctrine, original sin refers to the sinful condition in which man is born and in which he is burdened with many resistances to growth and free development. We may ask whether, in the evolutionary perspective adopted in this article, the myth of original sin is also meaningful when applied to the world-creating process prior to man's entry into history. Since we have spoken of the religiousness of all of reality, since we have suggested that chemicals, flowers and animals have at one time responded to the evolutionary call, each in its own way, we may ask whether there is also a factor in this evolution that may be described as sin. Was there resistance to growth in the cosmos?

Not all the forces in the evolutionary process are constructive. If all biological species evolved from one form of life, why did some branches stop short while others continued on the adventurous road toward ever new horizons? If we can assign any meaning to what Teilhard de Chardin has called the "within" of every being, then any entity whatever is partly responsible for its participation in the evolutionary process. Some species seem to have been more interested in the development of their defenses than in the openness for new steps toward growth and interiorization in relation to the opportunities within the environment. Because of the specialization of their defense mechanisms, they may have deviated from the road toward greater openness and incarcerated themselves in the cage of their fears and anxieties. This is the process of ossification as opposed to that of spiritualization, which according to Teilhard is the fullfillment of the evolutionary process. Yet despite this trend toward ossification, man emerged on this earth. God's creativity in the cosmos was stronger than the forces of opposition.

And what a risk this evolution took! For man was the most dangerous of all animals! He would eventually be able to destroy himself as well as the conditions of life on this globe. The evolutionary summons did not shy away from this risk in the distant past. Why are we to think that this summons, this language of events, is not now calling us to another stage in the ongoing creation of man?

Can man collaborate in the creation of something higher than himself? Is such an undertaking sinful pride? Is it the negation of the submissiveness to which the creature is called? If we extend the meaning of this question, in the perspective of this article, to the whole of the evolutionary process, the answer becomes apparent. For the lower forms of life were all made to participate in the creation of the higher forms. There was no submissiveness in the cosmos; the various elements and organisms followed the evolutionary drift that carried them beyond their horizon.

The Need for Caution

Still, the warning of theologians, the anxious "Don't touch," does have important meaning in the evolutionary perspective here adopted. In the pre-human reality we see that every element is related to every other element. All are interconnected. This means that each individual being cannot behave at random, according to its "likes and dislikes." Whatever it decides to do will have a profound effect on itself and its environment. The inappropriate action will have its fearful repercussion, and the truly creative and suitable action will contribute to the greater growth of all. What is to be done in each situation is, therefore, to be determined by the integrity of the totality. This determination, however, is never static. New factors may modify a situation so that it becomes open to a new creative process. In this sense it is the situation that determines what is appropriate or not appropriate in the evolutionary process.

This description also applies to the human situation. Man may not change his environment indiscriminately; he may not play lord and master. He is lord over his existence and the creator of his future only to the extent that he recognizes the meaning of his situation, listens to the language of events, and serves the integrity of the totality. Because of man's long evolutionary past, something very deep in him defends the integrity of the evolutionary process and cries out "Don't" to any inappropriate trend in the creation of the future. This is the kind of theological "Don't" that the geneticist can understand. Here conversation is possible.

The Woman and the Fetus: "One Flesh"?

Rachel Conrad Wahlberg

A congressional committee that recently investigated possible hazards of birth control pills heard testimony only from male physicians and scientists; not one woman witness was called. So also with the abortion question; who is listening to the woman? One knowledgeable and articulate woman ready to speak out is Rachel Conrad Wahlberg, whose article (from the September 8, 1971, *Christian Century*)* brings into clear focus that basic starting point—what the experience of pregnancy means to a woman—apart from which any discussion of abstract matters is without roots. At one time a college instructor, Mrs. Wahlberg is the author of *Leave a Little Dust* (on the liberated management of the home). A resident of Austin, Texas, she actively lectures, conducts discussions, and participates in panels on all phases of the Women's Liberation movement.

. . . and those who make decisions of common concern must expect the decisions to be examined by those who are concerned. [John L. McKenzie in the *National Catholic Reporter*, March 26, 1971, book report supplement, page 1-A]

In discussions of abortion, the person most concerned is rarely mentioned: the pregnant woman. How does it feel to a woman to experience pregnancy and its dilemmas? What is the existential, experiential reality of carrying a fetus? Is the fetus "your own" in the sense that your hair is your own? Why or why not?

Consider the decisions you can make about your body. You

* 407 South Dearborn St., Chicago, Ill. 60605.

can drink to excess, you can smoke three packs a day, you can take drugs—in spite of the dangers of these actions. You can practice birth control, or choose not to. You can starve yourself or gorge yourself on food to the hazard of your health. You can have your body tattooed, your ears pierced, your nose reshaped. You can decide to have or not to have an operation. Your appendix is your own, and you can have it removed. Your kidneys are yours, and you can decide to give one of them to another family member in an emergency. You can even commit suicide. You are free to control your body in these and a hundred more ways. But if you are a woman?

I

If you are a woman, a human female, then, beginning at age ten to 12, an egg is sent every month from the ovaries through the fallopian tubes into the uterus. The egg, you might say, is your own, whether you want it or not. This is the way you are created; this is the system established by nature for populating the earth. So the child-woman accepts her reproductive system as her own, though not without exasperation, impatience, resentment. She may take some pride in the fact that she can have children. Just the same, she finds menstruation a nauseous bother all her adolescent and most of her adult life. There is no choice but to get used to it.

But consider what is involved. Over a period of 36 years in a woman's life, 400 or more eggs or ova make the monthly fallopian trip. If the ovum is not fertilized, it is expelled at some time between menstrual periods—even though it has potential life in it. And the uterus lining, unused for fetal nourishment that month, is expelled through menstruation. Many women are ignorant of this so-called ovulation process, are aware only of menstruation. But for every woman, it is one of *her own* eggs that travels through the fallopian tubes each month, the lining of *her own* uterus that is expelled each month in menstruation.

Now, there is a tendency in our society—perhaps in all societies—simply to view the female reproductive system as "a part of nature," along with the male system. But in fact the latter is in no way similar in inconvenience or potential hazards. For a boy, nocturnal emissions are bothersome, but not dangerous. For an adult male, when millions of sperm are deposited in the marriage (or nonmarriage) partner, the danger of pregnancy is once removed. He may feel concerned, but it is the woman's problem. It happens to her, to her body. The decision-making falls to her.

In fact, from puberty on, a woman makes decisions during her monthly cycle. If she has cramps, she decides to take medication. She may decide to avoid certain activities during the period. If she is involved in a sexual relationship, she makes a decision about birth control—when, what type—and seeks medical advice. It cannot be overemphasized that the woman's reproductive system is already within the orbit of her decision-making.

Thus, since the egg is the woman's, if the man's sperm meets it, the question arises: Whose is the fertilized egg, the zygote? It does not appear to belong to the man. If it did, if he had control over it, we would know that a brave new world had arrived. We would adopt the horse-breeders' phrase and speak of a child as "by Tom out of Sue"—Sue being a vessel for Tom's sperm, not a person who contributes her half of the child's genes. That is, the woman would be a mere incubator for the male's child. (Theologically, has not Mary been presented in this fashion—as if Mary's ovum really made no contribution to Jesus, as if the Holy Spirit and a nameless humanity mysteriously combined to form the human-divine Jesus? Of course, when this dogma was formulated, the genetic contribution of male and female was not yet understood and the greater concern was with paternity.)

However, to the woman who experiences the monthly

cycle, the fertilized egg is still *her* monthly egg. True, as it attaches to the uterus and cell division begins, its human potential becomes real, both theoretically and biologically. But existentially the case is quite different. Uterine attachment and cell division happen silently. No bugle blows, no one knows—not even the woman. There is only, a week or so after the sexual act at ovulation time, a missed period. There is only an awareness of possibilities.

II

How does a woman feel when she suspects the presence in her womb of the zygote? First, she considers the delay in menstruation. Almost every woman will run late occasionally in a 28–30 day cycle. Even missing a month or several months may not mean that she is pregnant. So at first she worries about the date. Did she count incorrectly? (Few women mark a calendar unless they are intent on becoming pregnant or are counting for birth control.) After years of counting, the date of her last period becomes a blur. Also, perhaps she desires or rejects childbearing. She wants the period or she doesn't—or, paradoxically, it can be both/and. She wants a child but hadn't planned it now. A woman never "wants" a period except to assure her that she is not pregnant.

But note: as yet she has no feeling of a-person-within-me. There is nothing to see, nothing to feel. Only the missed period (a minority of women experience other symptoms, but in many cases these must be attributed to causes other than pregnancy). The situation can be tantalizing—hopeful or frightening. If she goes to a doctor, he may perform a test to confirm a possible pregnancy. However, if she is married, he will probably recommend her waiting until the second missed period to determine her situation. Thus for weeks she may exist in a limbo of not knowing, a state of mental-emotional concern and anguish.

If she tells no one, neither husband nor lover, doctor nor friend, she can put off facing her dilemma and bolster her sense of being in control. She is a whole person, with a certain question, a certain puzzle in her mind. Since she has missed a period, she knows that she may be "with child" (that biblical term has more meaning for the last months of pregnancy when she feels bulk and movement); but just now she may refuse to accept the possibility, so that she can still feel that she is in control.

If the woman does not confide in anyone, she can live in this limbo for quite a while. She may have a feeling of: If I don't let on, it will go away. (A friend of mine convinced herself for four months that her fifth pregnancy was a tumor.) On the other hand, she may be delighted over the prospect of having a baby, but hold off telling in order to surprise family and friends. All her time in "limbo" she feels she is one individual, one person—a woman with an interior condition, an interior knowledge, that no one can see or share.

But once aware that there is a knot, a mass within her, she must come out of limbo. She knows now that the egg was fertilized, that she missed her period because the uterus lining is nourishing a fetus. She realizes now that a parasite is living in her and feeding on her, is enclosed by her, a being entirely subhuman, entirely dependent on her.

Most discussions of abortion ignore this personal angle—the experiential, existential reality of a parasite within. Impersonally—medically, morally, legally—there may seem to be two entities, the woman and the fetus. But for the woman there is one entity, her body—me. *To her, the fetus seems to be a part of her own body.*

In a very real sense, the female body *is* an incubator growing a parasite. But while commercial incubators are external to that which is incubated, the human or animal female incubator is itself fed upon, is itself a part of the life-giving, life-consuming process. The parasitical aspect is reflected in the fact that a mother's health can be dragged down during pregnancy if she is not getting the proper nourishment. Mysteriously, the fetus feeds on the nourishment of her body without her knowledge or consent.

Has mankind in any period of history truly given thought to the fact that the fetus feeds on the mother's body without any consideration for her needs? Who is the victim here? In poverty-stricken areas, in countries where people are starving, the pregnant mother's food is converted to the needs of the fetus, and the nursing mother becomes emaciated as the breast gives up the nourishment of her body. There is a cannibalistic aspect here: the fetus actually feeds on the mother's body. True, this is nature, and is in one sense a beautiful process. Nevertheless, the fetus can drain the mother of protein and bone nutritives like calcium, causing loss of weight and health.

Is it any wonder that a woman wants to have the right to decide whether her body is to be used in this fashion? Helpless, the fetus feeds on the mother. Helplessly, she is fed on. Because of this interaction, she feels that the fetus *is* her own body.

III

There is nothing similar in the experience of the male. He can observe the woman, be sympathetic, defensive, judgmental, apprehensive. But he cannot ever feel the personal bodily involvement of having a fetus growing enormously within him, using, draining his body. That is why many men seem curiously callous and indifferent to the woman's involvement (though I must admit that even William Buckley agreed when Betty Friedan said to him on a recent television interview: "If you had a uterus in your body, wouldn't you feel you were more important than what was in the uterus?").

The woman feels both that the fetus is *she* and that it is *hers*. It is her *possession* since it is submerged in her. Thus the self-fetus relationship is unique; "it" seems a part of and uses her. Enclosed by her body, it can grow nowhere else. No one can see it or touch it. After a few months, it moves, evidencing life—but within her, the autonomous person. For nine months it is a part of her body. It never feels alien. According to current science, the body rejects foreign tissue. *If the fetus were alien tissue, the body would reject it.* This, it seems to me, is the most convincing argument that the fetus *is* a part of the mother's body until birth.

The enclosed organism—strictly a potential human, a subhuman, a nearly human—is not autonomous. It has no use of its potential senses. It cannot speak, smell, breathe, touch, respond to light. It cannot eat, drink, walk. Not until the last months can it move, kick, jerk, shift, respond to loud noise, all within limits in the incubator body. The fetus is not viable: it cannot live alone until the last two or three months of intrauterine existence, and then only under the most favorable, medically assisted conditions. By all these standards it is not a full human being.

IV

Thus it seems absurd to women that Grisez and others argue that "the embryo from conception until birth is a living, human individual" (*National Catholic Reporter*, March 26, 1971, page 5-A). True, it begins to take on person-characteristics, growth and movement, during the last half of pregnancy, but still only within me, within my body-world, my sphere. It cannot become a real person until it separates from my body during birth. Thus, *the fetus-mother relationship is unique, is indeed "one flesh."* Again, is it any wonder that the woman feels that the fetus belongs to her, is a part of her?

The fact is that the woman already has some right of decision over pregnancy. She may deliberately take vitamins and calcium, she may deliberately eat more and better food and avoid smoking or drugs, if she thinks this course will benefit the fetus. Or, she may neglect the needs of the fetus through ignorance—through eating poorly or not seeking medical care. She may diet to keep the baby small, or—trusting old wives' tales—she may "eat for two" to ensure a big healthy baby. Or, knowing that it may harm the fetus, she may smoke or consume drugs or alcohol excessively. Finally, she could, deliberately or inadvertently, take action to induce a miscarriage. Such action can be as deliberate as a planned abortion—and has never been regarded as shocking or as meriting religious or social opprobrium. (To my knowledge there is no law against willfully inducing miscarriage.)

Yes, the woman already exercises some control over the fetus. Thus, to the woman who does not meekly accept the situation, the question becomes: Can I decide to do something with this part of my own body, flesh of my flesh, blood of my blood, ovum from my ovaries—if I do not want to be a mother or do not want to have another child? Am I free or am I bound? Shall I bring on a miscarriage if I can, or get an abortion? Or, if I am unmarried, shall I have the baby and offer it for adoption?

Note the power implicit in this last question: she can offer it for adoption. She has the right to give this to-be-born life to another person or family, or to an agency which can place it with appropriate parents. In our society this is the unquestioned right of the *unmarried girl*. The married mother is not conceded this right. It is extremely rare for a married woman to negotiate with anyone to accept her child after she delivers it. Why does such action seem unnatural for a married woman, but natural, or socially desirable, for an unmarried woman? Partly, perhaps, because the married woman is expected to take her husband's wishes into consideration.

The crucial point for the woman is: she feels that if she does not have power of decision over the contents of her uterus, then the fetus has a certain power over her. It can take over her life—impose new duties on her, force her to quit a job and to give her time and energy to child care—a task she may not be ready for or may already have had enough of. In this sense, if the woman is not in control, the pregnancy takes control. She becomes a housing-incubator for a potential being who can change her life for 20 years. If she has no power of decision, she is undoubtedly being used against her will—whether through carelessness or ineffective methods of birth control—for procreation. Obviously, her will may cooperate, may coincide with her condition. But if it does not, she is in an oppressed position, the position most women have been in for centuries. She is at the mercy of her reproductive system.

V

It seems clear that the dice are loaded against the woman. In her lifetime her system readies several hundred ova for fertilization. Hence she lives for years with the overriding question: *How shall I avoid becoming pregnant except for the few times that I choose to have a child?* The male expels a few million sperm during every sexual act, but he doesn't suffer the consequences save insofar as he may have to support a child. The woman is trapped into dealing constantly with her procreative powers—and not just once a month, since she is never sure just when the egg is vulnerable. A woman lives defensively.

Obviously, for the average woman a safe birth control method is the answer to her 36-year dilemma. Unfortunately, many methods are ineffective or dangerous for some reason. Yet because the mature, sexually relating woman is always under threat, always battling fear, she is forced to consider almost every means of avoiding pregnancy: abstinence or "chastity"; constant attention to her chosen method of birth control; abortion; or having a hysterectomy or her tubes tied if she can persuade a doctor to perform the operation—

which he is unlikely to do until after she has had several children. A man can have a vasectomy whenever he wants, but a woman cannot have a hysterectomy or tube-tying on request.

Most women do not want to reject the fetus once it has begun to move. Ideally, abortion should be limited to the premovement period, the first 12 to 14 weeks. Incidentally, it ought to be possible for a married as well as an unmarried woman to give her baby for adoption, but this would require a reorienting of social understanding.

As a consequence of her feeling that the fetus is part of her body until gestation is complete, a woman faces two questions: (1) As an autonomous individual, do I have a right to make decisions not only about menstruation, birth control, sex relations, but also about what is in and of my body and seems to be me? (2) Since pregnancy is a traumatic condition which can change my whole life, how can I safely avoid pregnancy except for the few children I desire? Although in most marriages husband and wife will agree about pregnancy, I hold that women should have the primary power of decision because of three pertinent factors: the woman has the pregnancy—the man can't share it; the woman gives birth—the man can't experience it; and the woman is in general responsible for child care, not the man. Since women are ludicrously oversupplied with ova, the sexually active must have protection from unwanted pregnancies. To be free and not slaves, women must have power of decision over their reproductive systems.

Virginity and the Cosmic Christ

Sister M. Romanus Penrose, O.S.B.

In our sex-conscious time, the idea of voluntary virginity will seem to many a quaint anachronism at best—even when that idea is defended in terms of an *au courant* Teilhardian evolutionism. Sister M. Romanus Penrose, O.S.B., will not convince everyone, but her argument is cogent and warrants being taken seriously. It is her contention that consecrated virginity is a kind of realized eschatology, constituting "a major breakthrough in the process of evolution" because through it "the universalization of love—the spiritualization of love—is realized here and now in concrete form." Sister Penrose is vocation director for a contemplative community, the Benedictine Convent of Perpetual Adoration, in St. Louis, Missouri. Originally written as an assignment for a course in "Cosmic Christology" at the University of San Francisco, her essay was published in revised form in the March 1972 issue of the *Review for Religious.**

LAST YEAR when seven of us participated in the newly revised consecration of virgins ceremony at our motherhouse in St. Louis, we realized many people would question that anyone would want to give public witness to virginity at this particular time when the validity of celibacy itself is debated. We candidly discussed the possibility of our being out of it, of being anachronistic in an age and a culture which does not consider virginity a positive value. Since the consecration meant so much to us personally, we decided to probe more deeply into our own motivations and into the mystery of consecrated virginity itself.

* 612 Humboldt Building, North Grand Blvd., St. Louis, Mo. 63103.

We had no wish to criticize the rationale, discussions, and investigations that presently urge voluntary celibacy for diocesan priests of the Western Church. At the same time, we did want to bring into sharper focus the positive value which we feel is somewhat clouded by this issue. This article embodies the feelings and views of the seven of us who reaffirmed our vow of celibacy and asked the Church to accept this reaffirmation through a solemn consecration. I would like to share these thoughts with you as well as develop one particular aspect which I feel has special relevance for our own day.

One sister said: "The consecration speaks of faithful love in a special manner to our insecure and unfaithful age. As a consecrated virgin, I want to be intent on living my role well so that the power and presence of Christ in me may in some way help everyone draw strength to be true, valiant, and really free." Another said: "The consecration seems relevant for our time, which is characterized in America by meaninglessness and unhappiness. By the consecration, the virgin solemnly offers that which she has lived in joyous, undaunted love and proclaims unflinchingly her desire to continue living it into eternity." Still another: "Today when celibacy is so much questioned, I think this ceremony is particularly relevant, indicating as it does, that the seven of us do find religious life meaningful and are able to find fulfillment in it. It is something of a climax in my religious life and indicates my complete self-surrender to Him who first called me. I belong to Him and He to me—forever!"

One expressed it this way: "By the gift of celibate love, God's gift to me and mine to Him, I have vowed, dynamically fixed my will in a living, life-giving 'Here I am,' totally available, virginally empty, attentive, and attuned to the presence of Him who asks the question, 'Where are you?' Virginal love is love at its deepest level. It is my desire to respond through this consecration that *I am here* . . . from God. I am here *for* God, celebrating creation and life, and with joy and grateful praise, one with God's beloved Son in His eternal *yes* to the Father's love, alive with their Spirit . . . God is asking me together with every other man to *share* life . . . to be the grain of wheat which brings forth fruit for other men. Some share life through marriage vows and exclusive love. God disposed me psychologically to share life by religious vows in celibate love, i.e., in a deep communion of love with Him, and through that communion of warmth of trustful love and concern for all men."

A final comment was: "I see consecrated virginity, if I live it with enthusiasm, as *the* way of achieving the great, absolute good in my life. It frees me to pursue the 'one thing necessary'—total dedication to the Lord—with the totality of my being. It enables me to say to the whole community of His people, 'I am for you.' It enables me to say that love of God surpasses and is more satisfying than any other love and to concretize in dramatic fashion the transcendent element found in all true human love. I see consecrated virginity as a value of cosmic proportions. In a world which today acknowledges the evolutionary process as a fact, virginity constitutes a most important role in the 'building up of the earth.' "

It is the last quotation which I would particularly like to develop more precisely, for, it seems to me, it points out the crucial importance of virginity today. The current contemporary attitude toward voluntary virginity can probably be summed up in Sidney Callahan's observation: "A compulsively coupled society, such as that which marks the contemporary American scene, degrades and despises single persons who are not sexually 'fulfilled.' "[1]

I would like to suggest that this earthy attitude, which equates experience of genital sexuality with fulfillment, goes contrary, paradoxically, to another contemporary attitude which emphasizes incarnational theology. In fact, if we agree with Teilhard de Chardin's vision of the evolutionary process, we can more clearly see that voluntary celibacy even constitutes a value of cosmic proportions. He sees this whole process, which is a process of unity, as a movement of love.

According to Teilhard, this movement toward unification can be found even in the lowest forms of life. As the movement progresses, the forms of love become transformed and incorporated into a more complex synthesis (complexification). The original forms do not completely disappear with each new stage, but are transformed and elevated. In other words, there is both continuity and discontinuity in the process. As the higher forms of life appear, this movement toward unity becomes more complex; but at the same time, unity itself becomes more evident, especially as seen in the later stages of evolution: in the realm of sexual passion, parental love, and social communion. The advent of man in the universe provokes a crisis because of man's reflective power. This movement, which Teilhard calls divergence, though threatening the evolutionary process, is corrected by a countermovement of convergence that brings about a corresponding progress in consciousness. Increased consciousness, in turn, contains possibilities of both greater good and greater evil:

> It is precisely here that the theme of love emerges in all its crucial importance. For it is only love which is able to "cement" together the noosphere into a genuinely physical or organic unity and thus bring evolution to its completion, that is, to that stage of superreflection and superhumanity which is the necessary but insufficient preliminary to the Parousia.[2]

At this stage, Teilhard says, a universalized love is a biological necessity. This poses a problem for man, however, as it seems he can only love a rather restricted number of persons. If he tried to love everyone and the whole cosmos, he would most likely end loving nothing. The problem, which Teilhard himself raises, is also resolved by him when he tells us to look at the evolutionary process itself. In the earlier stages, the development of consciousness is concerned primarily with the interaction between matter and spirit and tangential and radial energy.

However, with man a certain independence from the material and tangential is achieved so that the movement of evolution begins to take place more and more in the order of the spiritual radial. It is as it were a spiritual molecularization which must occur and it is love (the highest form of radial energy), and of necessity a non-restrictive, nondivisive form of love, which makes such molecularization possible.[3]

Thus it is complexification in the order of spirit rather than matter which gives rise to the highest levels of consciousness. According to Teilhard, tangential energy will disappear and only radial energy, of which love is the highest form, will remain at the Parousia. Man becomes increasingly, but never totally, independent of his material base as evolution advances.

Such a universal love is necessary to molecularize the whole noosphere in order to achieve the Parousia, but it is also vital for the individual person who can only be brought to full personalization by involvement in the whole.

Although our individualistic instincts may rebel against the drive towards the collective, they do so in vain and wrongly. In vain because no power in the world can enable us to escape from what is in itself the power of the world. And wrongly because the real nature of this impulse that is sweeping us towards a state of superorganization is such as to make us more completely personalized and human.[4]

Other current writers have expressed this same idea from different points of view. Perhaps they amplify the specific details of self-fulfillment:

Love of one person implies love of man as such.[5]
In contrast to symbiotic union, mature love is union under the condition of preserving one's integrity, one's individuality.

Love is an active power in man; a power which breaks through the walls which separate man from his fellow man, which unites him with others; love makes him overcome the sense of isolation and separateness, yet permits him to be himself, to retain his integrity. In love the paradox occurs that two beings become one and yet remain two.[6]

If we want to conceive the community as a totality, a sort of "whole," then it will have to be a "whole made up of wholes."[7]

Thus, it is through the universalization of love that we discover our own uniqueness. We cannot be fully personalized without being totalized, that is, more participative in the whole. Teilhard believes this could happen only in an evolving universe where all things are organically related, where there is a solidarity and interdependence of all things with and upon one another. In a book entitled *Teilhard and Personalism,* Andre Ligneul allays some of the fears that totalization leads to dehumanizing collectivism:

Union personalizes through the gentle influence of internal forces of attraction, not under the pressure of external forces of coercion. This totalization differentiates what it unites, that is to say, procures for each one his optimum fulfillment and uniqueness. But only the unanimization resulting from the participation of each freedom will lead to a personal universe. The more persons are deliberately communitarian, the more collective forces will function conformably to the structure of free elements.[8]

However, how is it possible for man to achieve the epitome of universal love? Teilhard finds the answer in the personal Omega, Christ, who transcends the universe and is at the same time immanent in it. He who is both loving and lovable achieves this universal love by exerting a transforming influence over men that draws them toward the Center, Himself, at the same time that it draws them into unity with one another.

In short, a whole doctrine of grace is implied in the universalizing power of Christ-Omega over human love-energy. This is a love which man on his own could never achieve. It is charity. Charity, which is a universal love, is the word of Christ in man and it implies a transcending of all the limited forms of human love which, even when they are positively good, are still divisive of the noosphere because they are not all-encompassing. Christian charity, then, completes love-energy by universalizing and supernaturalizing it.[9]

And so it is charity that builds up the universe. However, before we can speak about love in its fulfillment, we must see love as it is in process. Only then will we understand the vital role virginity has in the process. Teilhard sees the manifestation of the power of love coming to consciousness within us in three successive stages: "In woman (in her love for man), in society, and in the totality—through the sexual sense, through the human sense, and through the cosmic sense."[10] He sees each of these stages of love becoming more profoundly interior, more spiritual, than the preceding one.

. . . little by little, love begins to reveal its own proper characteristics without however being able to disengage itself clearly from the mere function of reproduction. It is only at the stage of hominization that love in its fully developed form makes its appearance. Its true power is visible only at this stage. "Hominized" love is distinguishable from every other form of love by the very fact that its warm and penetrating light has been incredibly enriched. It is now no longer a unique and periodic form of attraction bound exclusively to material reproduction, but rather it has become a limitless and thereby restless possibility for contact through spirit rather than simply through the body. Its innumerable but subtle antennae pierce to the delicately nuanced depths of the soul in such a way that its attractive power leads to a mutual growth in sensitivity and ultimately to mutual fulfillment.[11]

The quotation above indicates that love manifested physically should express and create a *personal* union of spirit between the couple and at the same time lead them out of themselves, cause them to transcend themselves. This is the universal, spiritual aspect of human love. This is the "change of state" within the noosphere; "and this process is a step towards the collective approach of the human to the divine."[12]

This is the ideal role sex can and ought to play in universalizing love. At the same time, we must remember, the physical expression of love and the thing expressed, though related, are not one and the same reality. And the thing expressed, that is, openness, receptivity, and self-giving to the other, is more important than the expression itself. Donald Gray points out: "While sex can provide a point of departure toward spiritualization and ultimately universal love, it often does not."[13]

The same author discusses the problem that in human sexual love causes the crisis we have already seen in the picture at the stage of reflection in the evolutionary process:

In the concrete order of things sex is by no means an unambiguous reality. That this is the case becomes clear, first of all, in the fact that sexual attraction constitutes but a limited overcoming of the general repulsion which occurs with the appearance of reflection and which is concretely manifested in the tendency of each individual to close in on himself. Hence in and of itself it cannot produce that unitive energy which planetary molecularization requires and which only a universal love ("the cosmic sense") can provide. Secondly, there is a tendency for the couple to reenact at their own level that turning in upon themselves which is visible at the individual level. And finally there is the danger of seeking union precisely through matter, which holds out the possibility "of union as a lure" and which leads only to separation and multiplicity, rather than through the spirit which alone leads to genuine unity by way of synthesis.[14]

I suggest that consecrated virginity, vibrantly lived, contributes a breakthough in the divergent element described above, bringing into play the convergence necessary to usher in the Parousia. I would also pose a question: If we believe in the evolutionary process as envisaged by Teilhard and say that God's work in this process depends on our own, is it reasonable to neglect or minimize this particular area of the process in our thinking and discussions?

If we sincerely believe that man aids or hinders this movement, should we not take his responsibility in this area at least as seriously as we do his building up of the earth in other areas, such as technology, social justice, and so forth? Should we not speak of this process in terms of total growth, and is virginity not part of it? It is true Teilhard (at least in the sources I was able to use) never explicitly said he expected to have this eschatological reality take place universally in the realm of history. However, he implies it when he talks of the future as "an entirely virginized universe,"[15] and says, "it is in this way (i.e., through a shift toward the properly spiritual tasks necessary at the later phases of the process of evolution) that virginity will tend to supplant the state of marriage."[16] He seems to see celibacy and the sublimated sexual sense (the transcendent aspect of physical union) as the way of the future: "But this is particularly true of celibacy which spiritualizes love to the utmost and in so doing overcomes the ambiguities inherent in sex."[17]

It is not our purpose to suggest that everyone must become a consecrated virgin, or that there are no difficulties involved, but perhaps we can come to some conclusions. I believe in Teilhard's thesis: Virginity is the sign that that unity which the physical unity of marriage attempts to induce can be achieved here and now without the sign—through the power of Christ. I believe, further, that virginity is not just a sign of the Parousia, but is an integral and vital element in that movement which will bring it into reality. It seems logical then to conclude that not only will there be more virgins immediately preceding the Parousia, but that those who are married will be living more "virginal," transcendent lives at the time of that stage of development.

Today we see the mass media presenting sex as an item divorced from love. This is degrading to the person. We hear cries of protest about the validity of a life of consecrated virginity. It all makes us wonder if this is possibly a stunted area in the evolutionary process or if those who have vowed virginity are unaware of the full implications of their responsibility in this area. In an article entitled, "Teilhard, Sexual Love and Celibacy," Father Charles Freible says:

> Teilhard understands our Lord to have definitively authenticated celibacy as a human aspiration that had been maturing in the human soul. Consequently, in Teilhard's eyes Christ's celibacy must witness to the higher form of life toward which the human race as a whole is tending. In our Lord's celibate example, then, we have in fact a twofold witness: a "here and now" or incarnational witness to the essentially spiritual foundation of all personal union, because Christ actually achieved the deepest possible personal union with both men and women without there being any passion or genital expression of His love for them; and a "hereafter" or eschatological witness, which points to the eventual state of ultimate union of persons, both men and women, in oneness of being through love, in which "there will be no marrying or giving in marriage."[18]

To say all of this is not to deny the ascetical aspects required by celibacy. On the other hand, it is not to say that abnegation in this area is an end in itself:

> However much we stress—rightly—the relevance of God's transcendent salvation to this world, its presence in history, its transforming influence upon personal relationships and life in community, in brief, its cosmic meaning, it remains true that each of us, and the world as a whole have to pass through

death to resurrection and the final Kingdom. Man does not reach his true fulfillment in this life, even in a happy Christian marriage. And it is the poor and empty, the deprived and suffering, the humanly unfulfilled who are particularly blessed, because they have, if they but recognize it, a greater receptivity for God's transcendent gift, fewer obstacles to block their acceptance of it.[19]

Thus, even in the virgin's more visible witnessing of the unfulfillment which is the lot of all mankind, there are eschatological implications. Virginity implies dispossession, the necessary element for entering the kingdom of the *anawim*. The virgin says concretely in the flesh that in making oneself available to others on a more universal scale, we become more open, receptive to the Other in whom all fulfillment is found.

Those who witness to virginity in community have the special advantage of a collective witness. Hopefully, all the present-day attempts to create and foster community will put the witness of virginity into sharper focus and thus aid the process I am speaking about. It is Christian charity, universal love, that will bring about that final amorization of the universe. Virginity is to give witness to that community of love found in the Trinity and this is the love for which Jesus prayed: ". . . that they may be one, even as we are one."[20] . . . "I in them and Thou in Me, that they may become perfectly one so that the world may know that Thou hast sent Me and hast loved them even as Thou hast loved Me."[21] ". . . that the love with which Thou hast loved Me may be in them, and I in them."[22]

What might result if the witness of consecrated virgins was so cosmic that it shouted out to all loud and clear: "You are greater than you think. This love which you periodically experience as transcendent now is just a small foretaste of what is to come. Look, it *is* possible to live in total self-giving, in openness to others, in total free response to Love. And see: in living this life of love, we do not lose our uniqueness. Indeed, our individuality is enhanced precisely to the degree our love is universalized!" I wonder what effect this might have, particularly on the mass media, the current opponents of the celibate life, and on those good Christians who wonder what this Trinitarian life is all about anyway? What might result if this witness were given not just by individuals, but in a communal way, en masse, so to speak? Perhaps all this sounds idealistic? However, idealism has always been the starting point for any practical action. I believe the time is ripe for this message. As Sidney Callahan writes, speaking to a world presently crying for freedom and equality, plagued by despair, and looking for authenticity:

> Those who choose dedicated celibacy live the sign of incompleteness, of fulfillment to come, of aspiration to a more complete community and perfect unity . . . The affirmation of hope implicit in their life choice proclaims that the world community is incomplete, that now is not enough, that the status quo will not satisfy.[23]
>
> The practice of celibacy affirms that being a human being is much more important than one's initial identity as a male or female.[24]

Only a great love determined to face any obstacles will be able to accomplish this work. Yet we must always keep in mind that virginity is a gift. Charles Davis implies his realization of this truth in an interview which took place shortly after his own marriage. He insists that an intense prayer life must accompany a life of consecrated virginity.

> . . . Celibacy can only be really met by a love of God that is really mystic. There has to be the kind of intimacy with God that is not simply a commitment and an endeavor to love God effectively and to meet Him in prayer, but has a mystical quality which can psychologically replace the intimacy that is found with another human being.[25]

Such a life of prayer and deep union with God is necessary to enable the virgin to live a fruitful life and to avoid the ever present possibility of incentration, which threatens to slow up the evolutionary process:

> . . . universal love cannot be conceived of as a work of man but rather only as a work of God in man since it is identical with that charity which is the specific characteristic of the Christian phylum. This is not to say that Christ has not been active in the unification of the universe from the beginning, but only that at a certain stage of evolution His activity is seen to be that of an immanent-transcendent center of divinization. In other words, it is at the later stages of evolution that the whole movement toward molecularization in the spirit is seen to be a work of grace.[26]

To summarize, voluntary virginity, vibrantly lived, constitutes a major breakthrough in the process of evolution which will eventually usher in the Parousia. It constitutes this breakthrough because through voluntary virginity the universalization of love—the spiritualization of love—is realized here and now in concrete form. It brings into play the divergent element necessary in each major phase of the evolutionary process. The possibility of the virgin's closing in upon self (incentration), becoming a sterile celibate, is also present in such a radical choice; however, this possibility need not follow. A dynamic life of consecrated virginity also realizes the convergent element because it spiritualizes to the highest possible degree love ordinarily expressed physically in marriage. If lived authentically, such a virginal life expresses openness and availability in a completely human way. Some may say this in a different way: they may say virginity constitutes realized eschatology, that is, living in the here and now a life of love that achieves fulfillment without marriage or the giving in marriage. I say the elements are present in a life of consecrated virginity. It is for the joyous, available celibates to prove that this is so.

Notes

1. Sidney Callahan, "Sex and the Single Catholic," *Critic*, February-March 1968, p. 50.
2. Donald Gray, "Teilhard de Chardin's Vision of Love," *Thought*, Winter 1967, p. 523.
3. *Ibid.*, pp. 524–5.
4. Pierre Teilhard de Chardin, *The Future of Man* (New York: Harper and Row, 1965), pp. 124–5.
5. Erich Fromm, *The Art of Loving* (New York: Harper and Row, 1956), p. 59.
6. *Ibid.*, pp. 20–1.
7. Robert Johann, *The Meaning of Love* (Westminster: Newman, 1959), p. 28.
8. Andre Ligneul, *Teilhard and Personalism* (New York: Paulist, 1968), p. 36.
9. Donald Gray, "Teilhard de Chardin's Vision," p. 528.
10. *Ibid.*, p. 530, quoting from Pierre Teilhard de Chardin, "Esquisse d'un universe personnel" (1936), published in his *Oeuvres*, v. 6, pp. 90–1.
11. *Ibid.*, p. 532, quoting from Pierre Teilhard de Chardin, "L'esprit de la terre" (1931), published in his *Oeuvres*, v. 6, p. 41.
12. Charles Freible, S.J., "Teilhard, Sexual Love, and Celibacy," *Review for Religious*, v. 26 (1967), p. 289, quoting from Claude Cuenot's *Teilhard de Chardin: A Biographical Study* (Baltimore: Helicon, 1965), pp. 28–9.
13. Donald Gray, "Teilhard de Chardin's Vision," p. 534.
14. *Ibid.*, p. 533.
15. *Ibid.*, p. 535, quoting from Pierre Teilhard de Chardin's "L'eternel feminin" (1918), published in his *Ecrits du temps de la Guerre* (Paris: Seuil, 1956), p. 260.
16. *Ibid.*, p. 535, quoting from Pierre Teilhard de Chardin's "Mons univers" (1918), published in his *Ecrits du temps de la Guerre* (Paris: Seuil, 1956), p. 276.
17. *Ibid.*, p. 535.
18. Charles Freible, S.J., "Teilhard, Sexual Love, and Celibacy," p. 290.
19. Charles Davis, "Empty and Poor for Christ," *America*, October 8, 1966, p. 420.
20. Jn 17:11.
21. Jn 17:23.
22. Jn 17:26.
23. Sidney Callahan, "Sex and the Single Catholic," p. 56.
24. *Ibid.*, p. 59.
25. Doris Grumbach, "Charles Davis—What Next?" *National Catholic Reporter*, July 10, 1968, p. 2.
26. Donald Gray, "Teilhard de Chardin's Vision," p. 531.

Women's Liberation and Christian Marriage

Daphne Nash

An activist in the Women's Liberation movement in England, Daphne Nash is intent on exploding the long-standing complex of myths surrounding marriage and the family, particularly insofar as those myths help to perpetuate the oppressed condition of women. "Monogamous marriage in the form of the nuclear family, which the Church at present supports, is quite unsuited to the demands of Christian love, as is the possessive ethic which sustains it and the capitalist economy which it in turn sustains." Clearly, Ms. Nash's position runs counter not only to the prevailing ideology of her church, the Roman Catholic, but of society as a whole; nonetheless, it is a position which seems to be gaining some ground—viz., the growth of the commune movement. Ms. Nash is engaged in research at Oxford University for a doctoral thesis on the economy and history of the late Iron Age in Gaul. Her article, the first she has written for publication, is from the May 1972 issue of *New Blackfriars.**

Any serious analysis of the systematic oppression of women must focus the greater part of its attention on the structure and role of the family. For us in the West the prevailing ideology identifies as central to a woman's task in life the running of a husband-and-family, while for the man, his wife and family belong to the private, "unimportant" side of life—to his "spare time." We are taught to equate marriage with having a family, and a family with the bourgeois nuclear family of two parents and a few children living as a self-contained unit. In this guise the family is justifiably condemned by feminists and some psycholo-

* Blackfriars, Oxford, England.

gists[1] as the most immediate locus of the oppression of women and children. It has the complex function of underpinning the capitalist economy by being the consumer unit it depends on,[2] and of perpetuating both itself and the repressive economic and political system by being one of the most influential places (along with school) where children are brought to see themselves and the world in the terms of the prevailing ideology, and thus to become law-abiding citizens.[3] On top of this is the severe economic pressure on women to marry, while men can afford not to if they like. Working-class and many middle-class women cannot earn enough to survive on their own.

The means proposed by various feminist analysts for the economic, political, psychological, and sexual liberation of women always include the abolition of the nuclear family.[4] A Christian committed to the struggle for women's liberation must question the point and form of Christian marriage as it is normally expressed. In a period when alternative patterns of living in community are only beginning to develop in the West, it is obviously not going to be possible to do much more than raise these questions and look at them.

Marriage and Society

The sacrament of Christian marriage should be a taking up of an activity which is in a vital way creative of a human community, and its transformation into an activity which is creative in some way of a community which does not yet fully exist (the kingdom). Marriage should be a re-expression in this way of whatever sort of creative interpersonal relationship is most necessary for the continued historical progress of a human community. The sheer physical production of the next generation is obviously the first essential, and historically the basic relationship in question has always been some form of male-female union. By the time the Church was organized, monogamous marriage was normal in the advanced Mediterranean countries, and was publicly recognized as necessary for the economic and social well-being of the State. A large-scale reluctance on the part of men to marry meant a threatened loss of future citizens (especially soldiers): so, for instance, at the time of Christ's birth Augustus was offering extravagant rewards and remission of military service to any Roman who would get married and have children. The same connection between marriage (in this case, the nuclear family) and the State in modern times is clear from a *Guardian* report (December 31, 1971) on the programme of the Austrian Socialist Party Government for making money gifts to all couples entering their first marriages on or after January 1 this year. The programme "is not based on a particular need to stimulate marriages—Austria's population grew by an adequate 5.4 percent between 1961 and 1971—but on the notion that the Government has a responsibility to help newlyweds to establish a household." Here we have both the identification of marriage and birthrate, and the capitalist state encouragement of the nuclear family. The poorest couples get the biggest gifts for the purchase of "housekeeping necessities." The wide range of disabilities suffered over the ages by the illegitimate is further evidence of the importance to the state of preserving the primacy of the family in one particular legal guise.

Since the continuous production of citizens was a preoccupation with any community, women have in our tradition been confined as far as was economically possible to the task of bearing and rearing children. The greater the wealth of the head of the family, the more this was the case (culminating in the middle-class family of today). The high rate of infant mortality and of women themselves associated with childbirth (into the 1950s still the largest single killer of women in England) contributed to making the only socially respectable thing for women to do in life to marry and have a family. In most societies there have been religious celibates, and prostitutes; but these have never been allowed to be the normal careers for women. Unmarried adult women who are neither have usually been regarded as the objects of pity (old maids), derision (battle-axes), or even fear (witches). The archetype of the happy woman has throughout our tradition been the wife-and-mother (or Madonna and Child).

Monogamy now means the nuclear family, which has become a reactionary force in society. This was not always the case: compared with the polygamy of previous communities, the monogamous traditions established by the Jews, Greeks, and Romans were an advance. They brought the husband face to face with his only wife all of the time, and this provided a framework within which the status of the wife as property or sign of her husband's wealth could be questioned. When she was able to own her own wealth, the subordination of her position became more doubtful. Jesus' preachings on marriage presuppose and commend monogamous union, and were designed to fulfil the liberating potential of that style of marriage.[5] It is worth noting that guerillas in the South Arabian peninsula today are trying to have the traditional polygamy of the area replaced with the more progressive monogamy. The Church adopted this most advanced and also by then well-established style of marriage, and saw in it the paradigm of creative human union in society. Thereafter it imposed it everywhere as the only possible form of Christian marriage. It is time now to question the absolute rightness of this position.

The Family Myth

Monogamous marriage in the form of the nuclear family, which the Church at present supports, is quite unsuited to the demands of Christian love, as is the possessive ethic, which sustains it, and the capitalist economy, which it in turn sustains.

The nuclear family functions at one level as the shock-absorber for a whole system of structural contradictions in

Western bourgeois society. A married woman in such a family is strung between the conflicting beliefs that the Family Unit is all-important and self-justifying (hence the popular phenomena of Christmas fuss, "family spirit," cult of the Holy Family, family weddings, Keeping Up With The Joneses, the cult of childhood, or the need for Marriage Guidance Councils) and that as an individual she has some rights of her own. ("I have ruined my life for you and the children" is a familiar stage in family rows.) She is also torn between the mythology of her essential equality with her husband preached by both Church and State (marriage is only valid if contracted by the free decision of both partners; it is contracted out of love, and love only exists between equals; the bride signs her own name in the register) and her *de facto* loss of autonomy to him. (She becomes Mrs-her-husband, is no longer taxed as an independent individual, and thus is almost wholly dependent on him economically.)

That the Church has colluded with the State in keeping women in "their" place in the home is undeniable. (The Pope has deplored the women's liberation movement, and the synod of bishops let us know in December that women's role in the Church is not going to change at the moment.) Both understand and uphold the important function of the family in preserving and perpetuating ideology.[6] Both have vested interests in maintaining the timeless (antihistorical) myths about women and the family—that there is something wrong with women who don't marry; that a woman will find "fulfilment" in husband and children; that childbearing is miraculous and motherhood is beautiful; that the primary purpose of marriage is to bear and rear children. In many countries there are still State rewards for large families (France, for instance), while the Catholic Church still condemns contraception.

This complex of myths, like those about heaven and hell, functions to distract attention from present realities and invites psychological (hence individual) escape into a utopian vision. The myth, in proclaiming the inevitable rightness of the present form of marriage, exercises a profoundly counterhistorical force. Symptomatic of the underlying attitude we are supposed to hold is the reference to a woman's wedding day as "the most important day of her life," and its treatment as the end of the story, after which they lived happily ever after, but had no more adventures. (A far cry, that, from the creative, historical ways of love!)

Marx's famous criticism of religion applies also to these myths about the family, which are not confined to "religious" people, but are common to the education of all of us in our society. (One could almost substitute the phrase "the family" for "religion" throughout this passage.) "Religion is the general theory of this world; its encyclopaedic compendium, its logic in popular form, its spiritual *point d'honneur*, its enthusiasm, its moral sanction, its solemn complement, its universal basis for consolation and justification. It is the imaginary realization of the human essence because the human essence possesses no true reality. . . . The abolition of religion as the illusory happiness of the people is the demand for their real happiness. The demand to give up the illusions about their condition is a demand to give up a condition that requires illusion."[7]

This latter demand is one which a Christian must make and which will mean in the present context an attack on the nuclear family by a struggle for the abolition of the conditions that require it. This is a struggle shared by women's liberationists and socialists alike, and one which must bring into question the point and form of marriage for Christians: in the vast majority of cases in Britain at the moment, marriage is the point of institution of a new nuclear family, and complacency with this state of affairs only enhances the Church's reputation for backing the forces of reaction. Whatever Christian marriage is, it cannot be the celebration of a dominative, essentially possessive relationship as a prefigurement of the kingdom.

The Liberation Struggle

The subjection of women by men and the psychological blackmail exercised back on men by women has its roots in the very impossibility of our not treating ourselves and other persons as things at least some of the time. The first effects of sin and death in Genesis, chapter 3, are embarrassed consciousness of the body as a sexual object (3, 7: "Then the eyes of both of them were opened and they realized that they were naked. So they sewed fig-leaves together to make themselves loin-cloths"), and the institution of social roles for men and women differentiated on the basis of biological function. (3, 16: "I will multiply your pains in childbearing, you shall give birth to your children in pain. Your yearning shall be for your husband, and he will lord it over you." And for the man, 3, 17–19: "Accursed be the soil because of you. With suffering you shall get your food from it every day of your life. . . . With sweat on your brow you shall eat your bread.") The corollary of this is that it will only be with the abolition of sin and death themselves, which are a condition of human community in its present state, that dominative relationships in their various forms (e.g., racial, economic, sexual) will be completely overcome. (Thus Galatians 3, 28: in the kingdom "there are no more distinctions between Jew and Greek, slave and free, male and female, but all of you are one in Christ Jesus.") That the dominative mode of interpersonal relationship is at its most primitive and deeply rooted in the male exercise of superiority over female is recognized by such socialists as Branka Magaš: "With the disappearance of female subjugation all other forms of oppression will crumble. This will happen when women are economically independent, and legally and socially equal to men."[8]

In the process of the struggle for the final liberation (or the kingdom), the nuclear family must go, as being the most immediate site of the oppression of women at the moment.

But to make its abolition the primary object of attack, or, for that matter, to rely on a change of heart here and now by women (and men) to achieve the desired end (thus, for instance, Tove Reventlow)[9] is to mistake the means towards, and the result of, a revolution which in abolishing the present system of ownership will also abolish the family that system needed; and in removing the distinctions between a man's work and world and a woman's work and world, will at the same time make meaningless the differential in "male" and "female" character traits that supported the previous role distinctions (and which therefore seemed "natural"). There are only such things as "feminine" virtues in the present order of things. In engaging in activity at a practical level (demands for equal pay, day nurseries for children to free the mother for work, formation of communes instead of boxed living), we must not lose sight of what this is pointing towards. If we do nothing and only talk of the revolution, we shall never get there; but if we make the means into ends in themselves, we shall not necessarily get there either. Previous feminist campaigns which allowed themselves to be content with the achievement of their nearest aims (for instance the vote) are responsible to a considerable degree for the slow progress and present difficulties experienced by the movement for women's liberation.

One of the most difficult immediate obstacles to be overcome is that of convincing women themselves that they are not naturally inferior to men. Many articulate public women firmly believe that women as a sex have certain "natural" characteristics—ones (such as woolly-mindedness and house-pride) which if they *were* inherent in women *would* make them inferior. Anyone who doubts this, or thinks the whole women's liberation case exaggerated, should listen to a few editions of BBC radio 4's panel programme "The Petticoat Line."[10] It is extremely difficult, even for those married women who are engaged in the struggle for their own liberation, to make progress beyond a limited point. Without a change in the law, they are handicapped economically: if they have an income of their own, it is taxed more heavily than when they were single; and even if they *must* manage on their own, the law is weighted against them. "A widow who sues for damages for her husband's death is still liable to have her chances of remarrying assessed by the judge if she also claims on behalf of her children" (*Guardian* report, December 22, 1971). Even middle-class women, who are responsible for much of the progress being made at the moment, meet with a discouraging amount of ridicule for the personal efforts they make. They are considered eccentrics and so not to be taken seriously.

This reaction indicates a central point about women's position which must also be overcome before widespread progress is evident. Women are trained to be spiritual peasants, conditioned to working only for themselves and their family, and to thinking of other women not as the members of a class they themselves belong to, but as rivals. This individualism is fostered at every turn (e.g., the caricature of the woman jealous of another woman in the same hat, or advertisements for a washing powder that will make *your* children's clothes whiter than your neighbour's); I outlined above how the myths about marriage and the family themselves invite individualist escape. Juliet Mitchell[11] has shown how women working in public find it extremely difficult to see themselves as workers in the same way as their husbands, or to unionize. Even factory work is an extension of their individualist roles at home. Thus the woman who tries to take steps toward her own liberation is treated as an individual phenomenon. It will only be when women can see themselves as a class and unite for action on a wide scale that they will pose a real threat to the male ascendancy.

The whole point of present political action at immediate and national level is to bring about changes one by one that will eventually make it impossible for the capitalist system to function any longer. Feminists and Christians should be able to agree on that. One of the social and economic structures which is in the early stages of such change is the nuclear family, for such reasons as those outlined above. Alternative forms of community will become established where children will be brought up with attitudes to community and human relationships more and more different from the present ones as time goes on and new structures emerge. The Liverpool Free School is one such move in the right direction.[12] What constitutes the most important interpersonal relationship for a community's continued progress will in all probability admit of much more variation than at present. In a community without private property, where children are raised in common or by those who want to and are good at it (have a "vocation"), there will not be the need there has been hitherto for one person to be the "head" or paterfamilias, and it is for instance possible that the basic unit of a community would be the commune (perhaps half-a-dozen or more adults plus children). In this case, the Church would have to rethink the theology of marriage; it would seem countercreative in such a case not to allow the sacramental validity of the unconditional commitment of several adults to one another. The Church has existed through several stages of the economic and political advance of history—slave-owning antiquity, feudalism, and capitalism. Bound up as it is with the concept of private property, monogamy in one form or another has been the only absolutely necessary form of marriage so far. As the relations of property ownership change, monogamy may be recognized as only one form among others of the creative interpersonal commitment necessary for the well-being of society.

Christian Marriage and Women's Liberation

The exact form the sacrament of marriage will take in a changed society cannot naturally be determined in advance of the appearance of the new structures. One thing we do know about it is that it will no longer happen in the kingdom.[13] Marriage is connected with our present inability not to exercise power over one another. If Christians are going to continue to marry, and to claim for that sacrament the Christian character of scandal and challenge to the established order, then they must examine its point.

I have suggested that the main function of marriage is that of community-building. In the case of Christian marriage this must be a certain sort of community—one based not on the domination of one class or race or sex by another (which is as much as to say based on the failure of communication between its members), but on nonpossessive love founded on the actual communication that exists between human beings because it exists between man and God. To take the development of this sort of love or communication seriously involves, among other things, a serious struggle against the oppression of women. Thomas Aquinas explains the sort of love I mean thus: "Not any and every sort of love can be explained in terms of friendship, but that love which is accompanied by wishing well: I mean when we love someone in such a way that we want his good. If, on the other hand, we do not desire good for the object of our love, but rather desire its good for ourselves (as when we are said to 'love' wine or a horse or something like that), it is not the love of friendship, but some sort of concupiscence; for it would be ridiculous to say that anyone was the friend of wine or a horse. However, even wanting the good of the other is not a sufficient account of friendship: a certain reciprocity in loving is also required. A friend is a friend of his friend. Now this sort of reciprocal well-wishing is based on communication of some sort. Since, therefore, mankind does have a certain sort of communication with God, in response to God's communication of his *beatitudo* to us, there should be some sort of friendship based on this communication . . . now the love founded on this communication is charity."[14] (A similar point is made by Paul (Ephesians, ch. 5) when he likens the relationship between husband and wife to that of Christ and the Church.) The love required here, in seeking the good of the other, will include that of liberating women from the slavery of their present roles.

But the attainment of the community which is the full realization of this *communicatio* lies at the end of the struggle for human liberation, which has many stages yet to go through.[15] It must be the task of those who believe that the kingdom will be arrived at, to do all they can to further the movement in that direction. Every revolutionary movement needs at least some members who are determined to see it through difficulties, who are prepared to give themselves up to the struggle unconditionally, and who can be identified. Those who have received the sacraments of marriage and order share these responsibilities, and the theology of both is in need of development for the same historical reasons. The point of Christian marriage must be to provide the same order of support for the movement towards the kingdom as the family has always provided for the State, but in doing so to challenge and finally subvert the State and all it stands for. At one level this will be a matter of the production and socialization of children, the next generation, in some context other than, and critical of, the nuclear family. But a community at any stage in its development is more than simply the sum of its numbers. Without the present economically determined social pressure on *every* married woman to have children (and for the first time in history conception need not be the nearly inevitable result of sexual intercourse, while at the same time it is questionable whether it is a good thing for the population to rise at its present rate), women will be freed to devote themselves to any of the other important functions in the community, which are now treated as the preserve of men. It is to be hoped that when theology catches up, women will be able also to take a part in the Church's leadership. This public activity will not be a shirking of "marital duty" on the part of married women. On the contrary, not even the most determined feminists deny that there will continue to be children.[16] The point is that childbearing should no longer be the highest achievement of all women, as though women had a biologically determined "essence" anyway—a deeply countercreative proposal. It should be the task of married Christians now to find some alternative to the nuclear family (one keeps coming back to communes)[17] as the first step forward, an alternative not based on the dominative and possessive ethic of capitalist society, but on the principles enunciated above by Aquinas. Naturally, this will not be fully realized in practice (yet), but unless we start we shall never get there. Only if we take some such steps and go on from there to struggle at both local and national level for the liberation of all of us from the multifarious oppressions we suffer, will Christian marriage be experienced as the scandal and revolutionary critique of society that it should be, and instead of being the focus of the oppressed condition of women, actually provide a sound basis for the beginnings of our freedom.

Notes

1. E.g., Shulamith Firestone, *The Dialectic of Sex*, London, 1971; Juliet Mitchell, *Women's Estate*, Pelican Books 1971; Germaine Greer, *The Female Eunich*, London (Paladin edition), 1971; R. D. Laing and A. Esterson, *Sanity, Madness and the Family*, Pelican Books, 1970; and other works by R. D. Laing.
2. On this and other points which I shall be treating from a more specifically feminist standpoint than he did, see Bernard Sharratt, "Corruption Begins at Home?" *New Blackfriars*, February, 1971, pp. 69–80.
3. This lies behind the reasons Mr. Michael de Marco, a Bronx Democrat, gave for opposing the proposed bill to make it illegal to discriminate against homosexuals in housing or employment. "I think that policemen, firemen, and teachers are image builders for our youth. At least I hope they still are." (*Guardian*, January 29, 1972). Homosexuals in these professions would undermine the image of the "real" male character necessary for the maintenance of the status quo, at the same time as threatening the "father-figure" image of policemen, firemen and teachers.
4. E.g., Germaine Greer, *op. cit.*, pp. 219–238.

5. Bernard Sharratt, *op. cit.*, p. 79; Irene Brennan, "Women in the Gospel," *New Blackfriars*, July, 1971, pp. 291–299.
6. Thus when the Bishop of Derry appealed for restraint on February 2nd he addressed his appeal "to you all, and particularly to the heads of families. . . ."
7. Introduction to *Towards a Critique of Hegel's Philosophy of Right*, in Karl Marx, Early Texts, ed. David McLellan, Oxford, 1971, p. 116.
8. Branka, Magaš, "Sex Politics: Class Politics,"/in *New Left Review* 66, March/April, 1971, p. 85.
9. Tove Reventlow, "Women and the Liberation of Men,"/in *New Blackfriars*, July, 1971, pp. 300–304.
10. This sort of opinion is of course held by many men. One of the difficulties experienced in the attempt of students of Essex University and miners to cooperate in the miners' strike at the end of January was that the "recognition of the students' seriousness was qualified by the miners' divided attitude to the women: women en masse were seen as militants; in individual encounters the miners tried with difficulty to assimilate them to their image of women." (7 *Days*, No. 14, 2–8 February, 1972, p. 17). In the debate on the Anti-Discrimination Bill on January 28th, Mr. Sharples, the Minister of State, Home Office is reported by the *Guardian* to have said that "discrimination did not arise in employment in the vast majority of cases . . . men and women were not competing for the same jobs in a huge field of industry, including heavy engineering, transport, and coal mining. The majority of women were working in jobs which were 'an extension of their traditional domestic role' . . . women wanted jobs in fields such as nursing, food, shops and the social services. A survey published in 1968 showed that the majority of women were satisfied with their jobs." An extreme point of view on the same topic was that attributed to Mr. Ronald Bell (Cons.): "Of course women are inferior. They are second-class citizens and ought to be treated as such."
11. *Op. cit.*, p. 124: "Ask many a woman whether she wants equal pay and the answer is likely to be 'no.' 'It wouldn't be fair, men do heavier work, we don't want to *take away* from their pay-packet, they are the bread-winners, we work for extras.' " The author treats this subject in some detail on pages 124–131.
12. On the Scotland Road Free School see, for instance, John Hoyland, "Teachers on a Tightrope"; in 7 *Days*, No. 15, February 9–15, 1972. The Free School is Britain's first community school, and has 45 working-class children aged between 9 and 16. There are no rules, compulsory attendance, or formal lessons. There are five teachers, four with degrees. "But we don't regard ourselves as teachers, in that sense. What we are trying to do is to extend the definition of teacher, so that it will include anyone in the area. Lots of the kids at the school get most out of the people in the area. Lots of

people come into the school and do a few jobs, and end up teaching the kids. . . . Most of the opposition we get comes from teachers, particularly in this area, and the Catholic Church. The local priest spent his sermon last Sunday criticizing the Free School, though he's never been there. Because we won't teach religion there. But the place is more religious than lots of his schools are. They beat the kids. . . . They indoctrinate them, they control them, they suppress them. . . . I see state education as being inherently elitist, but we started the Free School because we believe you can't have a revolution within the state system. . . . The system is tied to society, and if society says tomorrow, we've had enough of their liberalism, now we'll start teaching other things—the teachers'll jump to it. They're a depressing lot." In Italy the school of Barbiana had similar success as an alternative, and a similar, liberating effect on the children, in this case peasants. See, on that, *Letter to a Teacher* by the pupils of the School of Barbiana, Penguin Education Special, 1970.

13. Luke 20.34–5: "The children of this world take wives and husbands, but those who are judged worthy of a place in the other world and in the resurrection from the dead do not marry because they can no longer die."
14. Thomas Aquinas, *Summa Theologica*, 2.2.q.23 a.1.
15. Cf. V. I. Lenin, *The State and Revolution* passim, but especially ch.V.2 ". . . the transition from capitalist society—which is developing towards communism—to communist society is impossible without a 'political transition period. . . .' "
16. Though some, for instance Shulamith Firestone, have some extraordinary imaginative ideas about the ways in which their production may be shared with women by men and machines in the future.
17. Bernard Sharratt, *op. cit.*, pp. 77–79; Germaine Greer and Shulamith Firestone have similar observations to make.

Psychocivilized Direction of Behavior

José M. R. Delgado

A leading specialist in brain physiology and behavior, José M. R. Delgado, M.D., has been deeply involved in the kind of research—controversial research, according to some—about which he writes. In his view, "investigation and manipulation of the physiological mechanisms of mental and behavioral activities should provide a better understanding of man's biological, intellectual, and emotional capabilities and limitations, and also should help us clarify fundamental questions about personal identity, consciousness, education, freedom, and the very purpose of life." Born in Ronda, Spain, Dr. Delgado received his medical training at Madrid University; he is now professor of physiology at Yale University School of Medicine. He is the author of *Physical Control of the Mind: Toward a Psychocivilized Society*, as well as numerous articles for scientific journals. His present article is from the March-April 1972 issue of *The Humanist*.*

Insiders and Outsiders: Reaching for the Mind in the Depth of the Brain

IN THEIR ATTEMPTS to understand man, philosophers and scientists usually function as spectators in the theater of nature, as outsiders who perceive the world through sensory inputs; they do not understand those mechanisms of the mind where all information is evaluated for the initiation of feelings, thoughts, and actions. Until recently, mental functions eluded scientific experimentation

* 923 Kensington Ave., Buffalo, N.Y. 14215. Reprinted by permission.

because cerebral activity could not be detected, measured, or modified by any known physical or chemical means. Behavior was investigated by simple observations: Human beings looked at other human beings, provided them with specific information or education, and attempted to estimate the influence of these sensory inputs on behavioral outputs. Even the process of introspection consisted of analyzing the effects of information received from the environment.

The essential link between sensory inputs and behavioral outputs lies within cerebral structures and involves neurological mechanisms, chemical reactions, and electrical phenomena that are absolutely prerequisite for every mental manifestation. Perhaps because these processes were unknown or unreachable, they were often considered irrelevant to understanding the mind, and even in psychology the brain was referred to as a "black box" outside the realm of investigation. This situation would be comparable to our being denied entrance to an automobile factory and, from the outside, being able to observe the delivery of steel, rubber, glass, and other raw materials, and the exit of smoke, refuse, and finished cars. As outsiders it would be difficult for us to assess the organization of the factory, the processes involved, and the machinery used. It would be even more difficult to understand the policies of the company, to predict future models, or to influence the decisions of the board of directors. If, however, we could place inside the factory a net of agents equipped with cameras, microphones, tape recorders, and other sensors to transmit information to the outside, our understanding of the internal organization and our prediction of present and future activities would be greatly facilitated. If, beyond that, our agents had the skill and power to influence behavior and decisions of the workers and directors, we on the outside could modify internal activities and influence the products manufactured.

Modern techniques for brain exploration give us precisely these alternatives. In many laboratories throughout the world, mechanical, thermal, electrical, and chemical sensors and stimulators are being placed inside the working brain. With these instruments it is possible to detect the synchronous pulsing of neuronal pools or even the electrical discharges of single nerve cells. We can correlate physical phenomena of specific areas of the brain with determined sensory stimulation of sounds or shapes, and we can identify certain electrical wave patterns as indicators of ongoing behavioral responses such as learning or problem solving. Microscopic amounts of chemicals—such as catecholamines or amino acids—have been introduced into a small cerebral area; and, depending on the selected substance and neuronal region, the intervention has been found to increase or decrease sleep, sex, appetite, or a variety of other functions. We are learning about the cerebral basis of behavior, and how and where human experiences are stored in the brain. Memory, for example, is somehow related to the stereochemical synthesis of proteins; richness or poverty of early sensory experience is manifested in the thickness of the cerebral cortex, in the submicroscopic structure of neuronal connections, and in the enzymatic composition of the brain.

Investigation and manipulation of the physiological mechanisms of mental and behavioral activities should provide a better understanding of man's biological, intellectual, and emotional capabilities and limitations, and also should help us clarify fundamental questions about personal identity, consciousness, education, freedom, and the very purpose of life.

Technology and Possibilities of Brain Control

The reception of a sensory input is accompanied by electrical and chemical phenomena that are detectable in the depth of specific areas of the brain. These phenomena are considered normal because they are activated by the organism's physiological portals of entry, that is, by the sensory receptors. Although the concept of normality is disputable, it is convenient to differentiate the effects of these inputs from those responses evoked by agents that modify the brain without sensory intervention. The latter may be classified in three groups: psychoactive drugs, psychosurgery, and direct chemical or electrical stimulation of the brain. In this article we shall briefly consider the last method.

The brain is like an ocean through which, by relying on instrumental guidance, we can navigate without visibility and reach a specific destination. Using suitable cerebral maps, oriented according to stereotactic coordinates, we can blindly but quite accurately place electrodes within any desired brain structure. Guided by micromanipulators, assemblies of very fine wires are introduced through a small opening in the skull. The terminal contacts remain outside the skin and are used for electrical stimulations or recordings. Surgery is performed under anesthesia. As the electrodes may remain implanted for months or years, studies can be carried out with completely awake subjects who are engaged in normal activities. We can therefore experimentally investigate human and animal neuronal mechanisms related to learning, thinking, and behaving.

Experience has shown that this procedure is safe and painless. Patients wired for months have not expressed concern or discomfort; they have enjoyed normal activities and returned to the hospital only for periodic examination. There are several medical reasons for implanting electrodes in man. In some cases of drug-resistant epilepsy, it is necessary to explore the depth of cerebral structures involved in order to locate areas with abnormal discharges and to orient subsequent surgery. Patients with intractable pain, anxiety neurosis, involuntary movements, and other illnesses have also benefited from cerebral explorations without the stress and confinement of the operating room. Actually, the use of electrodes represents a more conservative approach than destruction of portions of the brain performed by neurosurgeons in the treatment of neurological disturbances. In some cases, programmed stimulation may be able to replace lesions as therapy, thereby avoiding the permanent destruction of cerebral tissue. In addition to these therapeutic values, implanted electrodes are important tools for the investigation of neurophysiological processes of animals such as monkeys and chimpanzees.

The presence of leads connecting the experimental subject to the recording instruments has represented an obstacle for free behavioral expression and for long-term stimulation. This problem has been solved by means of miniaturization and telecontrol. The instrument called stimoceiver, developed in our laboratory at Yale, permits both transmission and reception of several channels of electrical messages to and from the brain, using frequency-modulated radio links. A more advanced instrumentation, also developed by our group, is the multichannel transdermal stimulator, consisting of integrated circuits enclosed in biologically inert silicon. This instrument is implanted subcutaneously. It has no batteries; energy and signals are transferred through the intact skin by radio induction. The subject, animal or human, may thus be instrumented for life.

In animals, electrical stimulation of the brain's motor areas results in well-organized movements that are indistinguishable from voluntary activities. Some of the effects are simple responses: flexing a leg, closing an eye, opening the mouth. Stimulation of other areas may evoke sequential acts of varying complexity. Excitation of the red nucleus in monkeys, for example, produced a change in facial expression followed by head-turning, standing on two feet, circling, walking on two feet, climbing, low-toned vocalization, threats, and approaches to other animals. This complex and ordered sequence was repeated as often as the red nucleus was stimulated. The effects produced were reliable if the situation remained constant, but could adapt to environmental changes. For example, waving the catching net in front of the monkey induced a precipitous escape, inhibiting most of the motor effects evoked by cerebral stimulation, unless the applied electrical intensity was rather strong. The conclusion reached after considerable experimentation was that behavior is organized as motor fragments that have anatomical and functional representation within the brain. These fragments may be combined in different ways, like the notes of a melody, resulting in a succession of motor acts such as walking or eating. The formulas of motor activity may be activated in a similar way by the spontaneous "will" of the subject or by artificial electrical stimulation, which provides an excellent opportunity for analysis of the cerebral mechanisms of behavioral performance.

Even more interesting have been the results obtained by stimulating areas of the brain that play a role in emotional responses. In these cases, the evoked effect is not a stereotyped movement, but a change in general reactivity toward environmental inputs. For example, in restrained monkeys, stimulating the tegmentum, central gray, midline thalamus, and several other cerebral structures evoked a typical offensive reaction with showing of teeth, low-toned vocalization, flattening of ears, staring, restlessness, and a generally threatening attitude. When the same areas were stimulated by radio while the monkey was completely free and formed part of a colony, the results depended on the hierarchical status and the social situation. Thus when radio stimulation was applied to the boss, his aggression was directed against a particular monkey, an unfriendly male, and never against his favorite female. It should be emphasized that the increased aggressiveness depended on the electrical stimulation of the brain; the motor details of aggressive performance and the direction of hostility were determined by the previous experience of the animal and by the location and reactions of his enemies. This fact proved that the emotional state of anger could be differentiated experimentally from the actual aggressive performance and suggested that they were related to different cerebral mechanisms that could be influenced independently of each other.

The results obtained by cerebral stimulation of some of

our patients agreed with these findings. For example, in a boy with temporal lobe epilepsy, electrical excitation of the second temporal convolution elicited an eightfold increase in friendly manifestations and in verbal output. The effect was highly specific because it did not appear when other areas of the brain were stimulated. While the increase in communication and in affectivity depended on the artificially applied electricity, the facial expression, words chosen, phrases used, and ideological content of the conversation were in agreement with the patient's education and mental capacity. His basic personality had not been modified; only his affective tone and expressive aspect.

These results introduce many important questions about cerebrobehavioral correlations. Could friendliness be related to functional activation of determined areas of the brain? May this activation be induced in a similar way by specific psychic messages and by unspecific electrical signals? Can we interpret emotional tone as a cerebral bias that will modulate sensory input from the environment? Obtaining answers to these and many other questions will require more experiment and intellectual elaboration. The results already obtained in animals and humans, however, show that we have the tools necessary to investigate the neuronal basis of emotional and behavioral reactions and also that we can influence psychic functions by direct stimulation of the brain. These facts indicate that the brain and its functional counterpart, mental activities, are within experimental reach. What is necessary now is a great effort to investigate the basic cerebral mechanisms related to the essence of man and to direct our intellect toward the understanding and control of our emotional and behavioral activities.

Limits of Brain Manipulation

The main (and fortunate) limitation of brain interventions, whether by surgery or the application of electricity or chemicals, is that they can only trigger or modify what is already in the brain: They do not provide information or skills. Electrical stimulation may activiate physiological mechanisms, but it does not create them. We cannot force a subject to fly unless it already knows how and possesses wings; we cannot teach mathematics by sending a few volts to certain neurons; we cannot implant ideas electronically; we cannot transform an organism into a radio-controlled robot.

We must realize that even during activation of the normal mechanisms of physiological performance, the nerve impulse merely initiates preestablished processes. For example, the voluntary flexion of a limb is triggered by neural messages from the brain, but it depends on a sequence of genetically determined events, including very complex chemical reactions of sugars and proteins, all of which result in the mechanical shortening of muscle fiber. Electrically evoked behavior is like a chain reaction in which the final result depends more on the structure and organization of the components than on the trigger. In a similar way, we could ask whether the finger of the officer pushing a button to launch a man into orbit is responsible for the performance of the assembled, complicated machinery. Obviously his finger, like the electrical stimulus, is only the trigger of a well-programmed series of interdependent processes; consequently, the officer should not take much credit for the feat of orbiting astronauts around the earth.

In addition, behavioral responses are determined by a constellation of factors among which brain stimulation is only one. A play of forces may result if the natural and artificial orders are contradictory. In one of our experiments, radio stimulation of the central gray in a monkey induced aggressive behavior manifested as vocalization, threatening, chasing, and biting other animals. But when exactly the same stimulation of the same animal was repeated in a different social setting, in the presence of a new monkey who dominated the stimulated one, it did not produce hostility; to the contrary, the monkey displayed submissive behavior such as grimacing.

These experimental facts illustrate the limitations of electronic control of the brain and should mitigate fears of its misuse. As discussed more extensively in my recent book *Physical Control of the Mind: Toward a Psychocivilized Society*, by stimulating the brain we cannot substitute one personality for another. It is true that we can influence emotional reactivity and perhaps make a patient more aggressive or amorous, but in each case the details of behavioral expression are related to the individual's past experience, which cannot be created by electricity. The classical methods of punishment and reward through normal sensory inputs are more effective than direct brain stimulation in inducing purposeful changes in behavioral activity. Ideologies, prejudices, beliefs, and customs are a part of the cultural setting inculcated during early childhood through normal sensory inputs; and they cannot be transmitted by direct excitation of the brain.

We must conclude that messages with complex meaning, the building blocks of personal identity, must reach the brain through the senses and that the power of brain stimulation is far more modest. The great potential interest of cerebral explorations is that they will provide the clues for understanding normal and abnormal behavior, paving the way for a more intelligent direction of education, and clarifying the biological possibilities and limits of the human mind.

Shaping the Mind by Operant Conditioning and Brain Manipulation

As demonstrated by B. F. Skinner and his school, operant conditioning, teaching machines, and programmed learning are powerful tools for shaping animal and human behavior. These procedures have been useful for educating normal and mentally deficient students and also as therapy for different types of deviant behavior, from homosexuality to phobias. Professor Skinner's recent book, *Beyond Freedom and Dignity*, represents a significant contribution to science and philosophy. I admire and agree with a good part of Skinner's ideas, including the necessity to design cultures and establish intelligent purpose in the behavioral shaping of the individual.

While recognizing the theoretical and practical importance of operant conditioning, I would like to point out that it is an "outsider" approach to the study of behavior: The scientist or educator offers a reward or punishment for performance of a determined response without necessarily being concerned with the intracerebral mechanisms involved. In Skinner's words, "Many physiologists regard themselves as looking for the physiological correlates of mental events. They regard physiological research as simply a more scientific version of introspection. But physiological techniques are not, of course, designed to detect or measure personalities, feelings, or thoughts." Although it is true that present methodology does not supply "very adequate information about what is going on inside a man as he behaves," I do not think that physiologists are merely interested in correlates of mental activity. With the new telemetric methods for radio communication with the brain, we have the tools to investigate not only behavioral correlates, but basic mechanisms. When movement is induced, affectivity changed, friendliness increased, or hostility manipulated in animals and humans by direct stimulation of specific cerebral structures, we are in touch with the neuronal circuits and functions responsible for these manifestations; and we can analyze their intimate activities. When we collect perfusates from the amygdala or the thalamus in awake primates, in order to follow the *in vivo* synthesis of catecholamines or amino acids during different behavioral responses, we may gain a deeper knowledge of the regional chemistry of emotions. When in response to a determined pattern of shapes or movements, unitary responses can be detected in occipital neurons, we are examining the essential events of visual perception.

It would be naive to look only to biochemical concepts and electrical fields for an explanation of the thinking process, just as it would be misleading to describe a painting only in chromatic terms. In the study of mental activity we must distinguish between the *material carriers* of coded information, which can be expressed as physical and chemical events of the neurons, and the *symbolic meaning*, which is molded by individual experience. The same symbol (for example, a red triangle) should activate the optic receptors similarly in different subjects; but, depending on a person's previous associations with this image, it may represent punishment or reward or may be neutral. The meaning is not in the material carrier, but in temporal associations among different carriers. We therefore need to correlate physical and psychological concepts that will supplement each other. Intracerebral studies can provide essential data for the understanding of how sensory input (education) is related to motor output (behavior). Ideally, then, when investigating the processes of human behavior, we should be both "outsiders" and "insiders."

Freedom

Behavioral freedom may be expressed as the conscious choice of one pattern of response from among several available alternatives, involving a rational evaluation of determinants and consequences. Biological, psychological, social, and economic factors form part of the situation to be evaluated. Accordingly, if we do not have money or proper clothing, we may be barred from access to a fancy restaurant; or from a smorgasbord table full of appetizing dishes, we may select varying amounts of several kinds of food, according to their aspect and our taste, hunger, mood, company, and other factors.

Automatism, on the other hand, is the antithesis of freedom: It is a response determined by the rigidity of the mechanisms involved; it requires a minimum of awareness, choice, or rationality. For example, the pupil constricts when exposed to light and dilates in darkness.

Freedom of action is relative, because it is determined and limited by the functional characteristics of supporting neurological mechanisms. Individual responses are a reaction to sensory stimulation and are patterned according to the frame of reference constructed within each individual by his past learning and experiences. Freedom is certainly a choice, but the number of choices is limited; the reasons for the choice are within the limits of rationality, and the performance is in agreement with biological laws and acquired skills. For example, I do not have the freedom to talk a language that I do not know, nor can I see if I am blind.

Freedom is also related to multiplicity of available choices and to technology. Primitive man was bound to a small territory and always had to search for food, while today we can travel to distant lands, taste exotic foods and live in sophisticated homes, enjoy the music of many cultures, and communicate instantaneously with any corner of the world. In addition, we enjoy the freedom of a greater awareness, the luxury of thinking, studying, exploring, comparing, and deciding. This is perhaps the highest quality of man and the most important function of the human brain: the rational evaluation of multifactorial situations in order to plan a strategy and to follow paths of action oriented toward pre-established aims, directing the forces and resources of nature, and educating the functions and development of our own neurons. Freedom is not a spontaneous and natural result of brain physiology, but the sophisticated product of civilization, education, and the humanization of man. It is increased by education. The neuronal mechanisms of rationality, the elements of knowledge, the evaluation of received information, the flexibility of responses, and other aspects of freedom are greatly influenced by the educational molding of the brain.

Choice involves mental effort. A rational evaluation of possibilities and consequences is time-consuming, requires responsibility, and may cause anxiety. Too many choices are tiresome. In order to perform efficiently, the brain stores symbols and sequences of responses that later will be used automatically. For example, most motor acts are performed according to ideokinetic formulas. These do not exist in the newborn brain, but are learned slowly by trial and error and then stored in memory. Thus, learning to walk is a tedious process, begun with clumsy movements and precarious equilibrium, and it occupies many months of a baby's life. After the formulas for performance are learned, however, they are used without awareness. Behavioral freedom requires a balance between this kind of automatic performance and conscious choice. To learn to walk we do not need to know about muscle spindles, the cerebellum, or cardiovascular adaptation. But for a scientifically sound program of children's education or rehabilitation, or for the diagnosis and therapy of walking disturbances, we need to know as much as possible about the biological mechanisms involved.

Liberal societies are based on the principle of self-determination. They assume that each person is born free and has the right and ability to develop his own mind, shape his own behavior, construct his own ideology, and express his personality without external pressures or indoctrination. The role of education is to help natural development without trying to change the individual. Privacy has a high priority, including its intellectual, emotional, material, and territorial aspects. Personal freedom is limited only when there is interference with the rights of others.

This nonrestrictive orientation has great appeal, especially for those educated in liberal societies; but unfortunately its assumptions are not supported by neurophysiological or psychological studies of intracerebral mechanisms. While an infant may have the theoretical right to "be free," he has neither the option nor the biological mechanisms for free behavior. For his brain lacks the stored information, neuronal circuitry, and functional keyboards that are prerequisites for the formulation of choices. The brain per se with all its genetic determination is not sufficient for the development of a mind. Mental structure depends on external information that will be stored as symbolic codes with material traces carved in the proteic flesh of the neurons; to evaluate sensory messages and determine a course of action, one must correlate present information with past experience. This fact is rather important, because without a frame of reference, evaluation of reality is not possible, and a frame of reference is not provided by the genes. The empty brain of the newborn lacks the necessary information and neuronal mechanisms to process the almost infinite number of inputs from the environment. Since only a limited number are used to structure each individual, their initial selection depends on chance and on such variables as the presence and behavior of parents and teachers. During the early years of childhood, the individual is unable to search independently for alternatives. Until our capacity for intelligent choice, or even resistance, has emerged, our personality is structured in a rather automatic way.

Personal freedom, then, is not a biological gift, but a mental attribute that must be acquired and cultivated. To be free is not to satisfy sexual instincts, to grow long hair, or to kill someone who annoys us. It requires the recognition of biological drives, the understanding of their underlying mechanisms, and the intelligent direction of behavior. Our task is not to discover a "true" personality, because the search for absolute values is fantasy. Rather, we must investigate the origin, reception, intracerebral circulation, and behavioral manifestations of the sets of values that form the relative frame of reference of each individual. With this approach, immutability of values and fatalistic determination of destiny are rejected. Instead of accepting natural fate, we gain greater freedom by using intelligence; we consider that ideological systems and behavioral reactivity are only relative human creations that can be improved and modified by the feedback of reason.

Who Is to Decide?

Our understanding of intracerebral mechanisms is growing at an impressive rate. Our power to influence the physical and functional properties of the brain is also increasing rapidly, and very soon we may be able to enhance or diminish specific behavioral qualities. Who, then, is going to decide the mental shape of future man, and what will be the bases for his decisions? Should we encourage individuality or conformism, rebellion or submissiveness, emotion or intellect? What are the risks of misusing this as yet incalculable power? What ethical principles should be established?

Rejecting the myth that each individual is born with a mental homunculus and accepting the fact that we are merely a product of genes plus sensory inputs provided by the surroundings, we approach a conclusion similar to that formulated so lucidly by Skinner: Cultures must be designed with a human purpose. Just as we have developed city planning, we should propose mental planning as a new and important discipline to formulate theories and practical means for directing the evolution of future man. We should not consider ourselves the end product of evolution; rather, we should try to imagine that thousands of years from now the inhabitants of the earth could differ more from present man than we differ from gorillas and chimpanzees. The key factor for our future development is human intelligence, which could play a decisive role in evolution.

In confronting the question "Who is to decide the qualities of future men?" we should remember that when a machine or an ideology has enough appeal and applicability, it will spread and it will be used. Our present task is to investigate the biological and mental capabilities of man and to evaluate the choices for future development. Then these choices should be made available to society and to the individual.

On one fundamental point I differ with Skinner: In cultural design, individual freedom should not be played down, but up. We should explain to the mature individual that a collection of frames of reference, including cultural prejudices, factual knowledge, conditioned reactions, and emotional settings, has been inculcated in him during his childhood; that this was done hopefully for a good purpose, but without his permission, because his brain could not develop in a vacuum of sensory inputs, and he did not have the appropriate mentality to make his own choices. Then he should be trained and encouraged to use the given building blocks of his personality in some original way, according to that unique combination of circumstances which constitutes his personal identity. It should also be made clear that we do not really own, nor have we invented, our frames of reference. They are simply borrowed from culture, although we may modify them by a process of intelligent feedback.

A Proposal

The present crisis in ideology, ethics, and human relations is in part determined by the internal contradictions of evolving civilization, including the lack of balance between rapid technological or material evolution and the slow pace of mental evolution. This imbalance is partly due to methodological problems. Study of the essential and continuous dependence of the mind on sensory reception will favor man's social integration, because it demonstrates that we cannot live alone and that our mental survival depends upon a constant stream of information from the environment. At the same time, exploration of the genetic, environmental, and intracerebral elements that determine mental structure will favor the intelligent selection of these elements and thus increase the basis for individual differentiation and personal freedom.

What I propose is the adoption of a strategy for mental planning. The project of conquering the human mind could be a central theme for international cooperation and understanding, because its aim is to know the mechanisms of the brain that make all men behave and misbehave, give us pleasure and suffering, and promote love and hate. The differences in genetic potential among men are magnified grotesquely, like shadows on a wall, by their educational environment. Even if political ideas, cultural values, and behavioral reactivity vary, the basic physical, intellectual, and emotional needs of men are the same; and they must have similar neurophysiological mechanisms. Hate and destruction are not functional properties of the brain, but elements introduced through sensory inputs; they originate not within the person, but in the environment.

The Freedom to Die

Daniel Maguire

Calling into question much of the "conventional wisdom" about death and dying—notions that tend to be simplistic and absolutist—Daniel Maguire examines four different dying situations and comes to conclusions that may seem surprising, particularly for a Roman Catholic. For example, in regard to certain cases involving conscious terminal patients, he declares that "direct positive intervention to bring on death may be morally permissible." And in regard to suicide: ". . . it may not be excluded that direct self-killing may be a good moral action, in spite of the strong presumptions against it." Dr. Maguire is associate professor of theology at Marquette University. His article originally appeared in the August 11, 1972, issue of *Commonweal.** Essays by Dr. Maguire are to be found in the following books: *The Paradox of Religious Secularity*, *Absolutes in Moral Theology?*, *American Catholics and Vietnam*, *Contraception: Authority and Dissent*, and *Toward Moral Maturity: Religious Education and the Formation of Conscience.*

Of old when men lay sick and sorely tried,
The doctors gave them physic and they died:
But here's a happier age, for now we know
Both how to make men sick and keep them so!
Hilaire Belloc

MAN IS THE ONLY ANIMAL who knows he is going to die, and he has borne this privileged information with uneven grace. On the one hand, poets and philosophers have gazed at death and proclaimed the significance

* 232 Madison Ave., New York, N.Y. 10016.

of death-consciousness. Hegel saw the awareness of mortality as such a stimulus to human achievement that he could define history as "what man does with death." Schopenhauer called death "the muse of philosophy" and Camus saw man's capacity for suicide as evoking the most fundamental philosophical questions. Poets have called death such things as "gentle night," "untimely frost," or "the great destroyer."

The average person, however, would rather forget it. This is especially true if the average person is an American since in this happiness-oriented land, death (outside of a military context) is seen as something of an un-American activity. It happens, of course, but it is disguised and *sub rosa*, like sex in Victorian England. Most Americans now die in hospitals. And they die without the benefit of the liturgies of dying that attend this natural event in cultures which accept death as a fact of human life. The dying process is marked by deceit, where everything except the most important fact of impending death can be addressed. When the unmentionable happens, the deceit goes on as the embalmers embark on their postmortem cosmetics to make the dead man look alive. Mourners, chemically fortified against tears that would betray the farce, recite their lines about how well the dead man looks when, in point of fact, he is not well and does not look it.

All of this does not supply the atmosphere in which man's moral right to die with dignity can receive its needed reevaluation. Nevertheless, the reevaluation must go on. Technology has already moved ahead of both ethics and law. As Johns Hopkins professor Diana Crane notes, "the nature of dying has changed qualitatively in recent years because of advances in medical knowledge and technology." These qualitative changes have dissipated older definitions of death, given greater power to doctors over life and death, shaken the never too fine art of prognosis, and presented all us mortals with options that old law and ethical theory did not contemplate . . . which options offer frontal challenges to some long-tenured traditions and taboos.

As if this were not complicated enough, the technological revolution has also caused a notable shift in our moral universe. The interplay between technology and morality is, of course, as old as man's first primitive tool. With technological advance comes power and with power, responsibility, and the question of whether this power can be used without intrusion into the realm of the gods. Prometheus, the philanthropic god who stole fire for men, was judged by Zeus to have gone too far. Bellerophon in the *Iliad* came to a sorry end for trying to ride to the Olympus of the gods and for thinking "thoughts too great for man." And Icarus, exulting in the technology of man-made wings, flew too close to the sun and perished. These myths, like the myths of Babel and Adam's sin, are relevant to the moral dilemma of inventive man. What thoughts and what initiatives are "too great for man"? Where are the sacred borders between the *can do* and the *may do*? Where does presumption enter into the knowledge of good and evil?

Medical ethics has long known the strain of this dilemma. Man has a tendency to consider the physical and biological to be ethically normative and inviolable. Blood transfusions were resisted by many on these grounds. Birth control was also, for a very long time, impeded by the physicalist ethic that left moral man at the mercy of his biology. He had no choice but to conform to the rhythms of his physical nature and to accept its determinations obediently. Only gradually did technological man discover that he was morally free to intervene creatively and to achieve birth control by choice.

Can We Intervene?

The question now arising is whether, in certain circumstances, we may intervene creatively to achieve death by choice or whether mortal man must in all cases await the good pleasure of biochemical and organic factors and allow these to determine the time and the manner of his demise. In more religious language, can the will of God regarding a person's death be manifested only through the collapse of sick or wounded organs or could it also be discovered through the sensitivities and reasonings of moral men? Could there be circumstances when it would be acutely reasonable (and therefore moral if one uses "reason" in a Thomistic sense) to terminate life through either positive action or calculated benign neglect rather than to await in awe the dispositions of organic tissue?

The discussion should proceed in the realization that the simpler days are past in which the ethics of dying was simple. Most importantly, the definition of death was no problem until recently. When the heart stopped beating and a person stopped breathing, he was dead. (Interestingly, the old theology manuals were not too sure of this since they advised that the sacrament of final anointing could be administered conditionally up to about two hours after "death.") Medical technology has changed all of that. It is now commonplace to restore palpitation to a heart that had fully stopped beating. Even when the natural capacity for cardiopulmonary activity is lost, these systems can be kept functioning through the aid of supplementary machinery. Heartbeat and breathing can be artificially maintained in a person whose brain is crushed or even deteriorated to the point of liquefaction. Heartbeat is no longer a safe criterion of human life!

This has turned medical people to the concept of "brain death." Indeed, Dr. Robert Glaser, the dean of Stanford's School of Medicine, says (somewhat prematurely, I judge): "Insofar as it involves organ donors and their rights, the technical question of death has been resolved, by popular consensus, in the recognition that the brain and not the heart is the seat of human life." Brain death, however, is not an answer without problems. A person with a hopelessly damaged brain could still have spontaneous heartbeat and respiration. Harvard's Dr. Henry Beecher asks the inevitable question here: "Would you bury such a man whose heart was beating?" And lawyers will be quick to tell you that the removal of vital organs from a body that has a dead brain but a live heart would raise the specter of legal liability.

All of this illumines the unsettling fact that death admits of degrees. Some organs and cells die before others. As Paul Ramsey observes, "the 'moment' of death is only a useful fiction." It may however be more fiction than useful if it leaves us hoping for a definition of death that will make it unnecessary for us to judge that a particular "life" should now be completely terminated by a positive act of omission or commission. Science will not give us a litmus test for death that will relieve us of all need for moral judgment and action. That day has passed and that is what makes for the qualitative change in dying and the ethics thereof.

It seems well to pursue this issue by considering four different dying situations: (1) the case of the irreversibly comatose patient whose life is sustained by artificial means; (2) the conscious patient whose life is supported artificially by such means as dialysis (for kidney patients) or iron lung; (3) the conscious patient who is dying of a terminal illness whose life is supported by natural means; (4) the case of self-killing in a nonmedical context.

First, then, to the case of the irreversibly comatose, artificially sustained patient. It is a useful beginning here to look at the remarkable address of Pius XII on the prolongation of life, given in 1957. In this talk, the Pope stated that the definition of death is an open question to which "the answer cannot be deduced from any religious and moral principle. . . ." He allows that in hopelessly unconscious patients on respirators "the soul may already have left the body," and he refers to such patients by the ambiguous but interesting term "virtually dead." The Pope points out that only ordinary means need be used to preserve life; and he supplies a broad definition of this slippery term, saying that ordinary means are "means that do not involve any grave burden for oneself or another." The Pope is dealing with the unconscious patient of whom it can be said that "only automatic artificial respiration is keeping him alive." In these hopeless cases, the Pope concludes that after several days of unsuccessful attempts, there is no moral obligation to keep the respirator going.

The respirator is, of course, an extraordinary means, especially when it is used on the irreversibly unconscious. For years now, theologians have also argued that even intravenous feedings in this type of case are extraordinary and may be discontinued. (Law lags behind ethics on this.) I would argue further that in such a case where the personality is permanently extinguished, one needs a justifying cause to continue artificial, supportive measures. To maintain bodily life at a vegetative level without cause is irrational, immoral, and a violation of the dignity of human life. It is a burden on the family; also, there may be need to allocate these medical resources to curable awaiting patients. It is, moreover, macabre, irreverent, and crudely materialistic to preserve by medical pyrotechnics the hopeless presence of what could best be described as a breathing corpse. Of these cases, when the patient is "irretrievably inaccessible to human care," Paul Ramsey says quite correctly that it is "a matter of complete indifference whether death gains the victory over the patient in such impenetrable solitude by direct or indirect action."

One reason that clearly justifies maintaining this kind of life is to make possible the donation of organs, since the human body thus sustained is considered to be the best possible tissue bank. Death, however, should first be declared, and the law should be pushed to update itself to allow for this. Probably our society is not prepared to grant that the organs in such instances should, by eminent domain, be allocated to those who need them. Through cultural conditioning and taboo, we are still disposed to prefer the "rights" of the dead to the needs of the living in this regard, and few people even carry donor cards now legal and available in all states. Thus the immoral waste of tissue that could be "a gift of life."

Our second case concerns the conscious patient whose life

is artificially supported. This is a broad category and could be stretched to include those who attribute their perdurance to superabundant dosages of Vitamin C and E. We are thinking, rather, of those who are alive thanks to dialysis or an iron lung. As medicine advances, this category will expand.

In assessing the moral right of such patients to die, one might be tempted to repair to the facile distinction between ordinary and extraordinary means. By the papal definition of ordinary means ("grave burden for oneself or another"), both dialysis and the iron lung are extraordinary. Thus the patients involved would appear to be under no obligation to continue in this kind of therapy and would seem free to discontinue the treatment and die.

We must, however, avoid the simplistic allurements of a one-rubric ethics. There is more involved here than the patient and the extraordinary means. We must (as does the papal teaching cited) speak also of the patient's obligations of social justice and charity, remembering that an individualistic, asocial ethics has also infected medical morality.

We have all heard much of the redemptive power of suffering. Unfortunately, the pieties of the past often interpreted this in accord with primitive myths of vindication which implied that pain and bloodshed of themselves had an atoning power. These myths, replete as they may be with sado-masochistic elements, have had an enormous influence both on Christology and Christian asceticism, attributing a positive per se value to suffering. Such a value suffering does not have, but rather assumes its meaning, value, or disvalue from the concrete circumstances of the sufferer.

In this sense there *can* be a redemptive value to suffering. Take the example of a kidney patient who has not had a successful transplant. Could he not see his plight as a vocation? His disease can become a rostrum, and he could become part of something that is needed . . . a lobby of the dying and the gravely ill. To be more specific, this nation which has borne him is also ill. Its priorities are out of joint.

It has, by morbid selection, chosen for itself what Richard Barnet calls "an economy of death." Its heart is so askew that only if dialysis could be shown to have *military* significance would it receive the government and private funding it desperately needs. Many illnesses could now be contained if the nation had given the zeal and the budget to life that it now gives to death.

The gravely ill with their unique credentials could do more here than they realize. By working creatively with politicians, national health organizations, medical and legal societies, news media, writers, etc.—and in ways as yet unthought of, which their healthy imaginations will bring forth—the lobby of the dying and the gravely ill could become a healing force in society. Man's nature is still so barbarous that the well attend more to the well than to the sick. Great obligations, therefore, devolve upon the sick. The well need the sick more than the well know.

Still, concerning persons in the category here discussed, if their artificially supported life becomes unbearable, they have a right to discontinue treatment; and we owe them in justice and in charity the direct or indirect means to leave this life with the dignity, comfort, and speed which they desire.

What then of the conscious, terminal patient whose life systems are functioning naturally? May he in any circumstance take direct, positive action to shorten his dying trajectory, or is the natural course of his disease ethically normative in an absolute sense? Those who would deny the moral right to direct acceleration of the death process will adduce an "absolute" principle such as the unconditional inviolability of innocent human life. This is taken to mean that innocent life may in no circumstance be terminated by direct, positive action.

John Milhaven, in an important 1966 *Theological Studies* article, notes the tendency simply to proclaim this inviolability principle and work from there in right-to-life cases. He cites the failure of those who do this to indicate "the reasons that prove there is an absolute inviolability, holding under all circumstances." And he asks the fair and telling question: "How do we know this?" In point of fact, I submit that we do not know this because it is not knowable.

Those who use the principle accept no burden of proof and offer only a fideistic assertion. They present the principle without proof, as self-evident. In ethics, however, only the most generic propositions are self-evident, such as "do good and avoid evil"; "to each his own." The *evidence* emerges from the mere understanding of the terms. Such statements are universally true because they lack particularizing and complicating content.

Practical principles such as the one on direct termination of innocent life must be proved, and the proof must come from wherever moral meaning is found; that is, it must come from a knowledge of the morally significant empirical data, the consequences, the existent alternatives, the unique circumstances of person, place and time, etc. Moral meaning is found not just in principles, but in all the concrete circumstances that constitute the reality of a person's situation; and the principles themselves are rooted in empirical experience and must be constantly rewashed in an empirical bath to check their abiding validity.

To say that something is morally right or wrong in all possible circumstances implies a divine knowledge of all possible circumstances and their moral meaning. To say that something is universally good or bad regardless of circumstances is non-sense, for it is to say that something is *really* good or bad regardless of the *reality-constituting* circumstances.

An attempt can be made to base the "no direct killing of innocent life principle" on the reality of expected intolerable consequences. This is the cracked dike argument. *Après moi le déluge!* If *X* is allowed, then *Y* and *Z* and everything else will be allowed. This is a kind of ethical domino theory which has the deficiencies of any domino theory. It ignores the real meaning of the real differences between *X*, *Y*, and *Z*.

Good ethics is based on reality and makes real distinctions where they are real differences. It is, furthermore, fallacious to say that if an exception is allowed, it will be difficult to draw the line and therefore no exception should be allowed. It has been said quite rightly that ethics like art is precisely a matter of knowing where to draw lines.

Therefore, with regard to the principle in question, we can say that its absoluteness is, at the very least, doubtful. And then in accord with the hallowed moral axiom *ubi dubium ibi libertas* (where there is doubt there is liberty), we can proclaim moral freedom to terminate life directly in certain cases. It would perhaps be better to put it in terms of Aristotelian-Thomistic moral theory. This principle, like every practical moral principle, is valid most of the time (*in pluribus*), but in a particular instance (*in aliquo particulari*) it may not be applicable.

To apply this whole discussion to the case of conscious terminal patients, it can be said that in certain cases, direct positive intervention to bring on death may be morally permissible. The decision, of course, should not ignore issues of social responsibility and opportunity alluded to in the preceding case. The patient must consider also his cultural and legal context, the mind-set of insurance companies, and the ability of others to cope with the voluntary aspects of his death. He must also beware lest he is yielding to societal pressures to measure human dignity in terms of utility or to create the illusion that sickness and death are unreal.

To repeat, therefore, direct action to bring on death in the situation described here may be moral. The absolutist stance opposed to this conclusion must assume the burden of proof —an impossible burden, I believe.

Finally, to self-killing in a nonmedical context. It is estimated that more than eighty Americans a day kill themselves. Jacques Choron calculates that between six and seven million living Americans have attempted suicide and that 25 percent of these will try again and many will succeed. From a moral viewpoint it may be said that an enormous majority of these cases represent unmitigated tragedy. Most suicides flow from a loss of the vital ingredients of human life, hope and a supportive loving community. Studies show the suicide as a lonely, desperate person. His act is *The Cry for Help,* the title of a book on attempted suicide by Farberow and Schneidman. Eighty percent of all suicides signal their intentions in advance, apparently by way of final, desperate pleading. Contrary to the rationalizing myth, most suicides are not psychotic. Alcoholism and drug use are, of course, not unrelated to the suicidal syndrome.

The incidence of suicide in certain groups is revealing. Suicide rates among blacks and Indians in this nation are rated as of epidemic proportions. Two to three times more women than men attempt suicide. Suicide increases in socially disorganized communities, and the rate of successful suicide among divorced persons is remarkably high. There can be no doubt that most suicides are an indictment of the surviving community, which failed to give the possibility of life to its suicidal victims.

The prime moral reaction to suicide should be to attack the causes that yield such bitter fruit. Those of Christian persuasion should be in the forefront here. For Christians, the loss of hope is apostasy, and to contribute to the loss of hope in others is the elementary Christian sin. Dietrich Bonhoeffer judged suicide severely from the perspective of Christian faith: "It is because there is a living God that suicide is wrongful as a sin of lack of faith." He did, however, realize that suicide is not univocal. Though usually akin to murder, "it would be very short-sighted simply to equate every form of self-killing with murder." Some suicides could be highly motivated, and Bonhoeffer was inclined to suspend judgment with regard to these because "here we have reached the limits of human knowledge." Unless we do ethics by taboo, however, we must do more than suspend judgment. We must also discuss the possibility of objectively moral suicide. The discussion here relies on the points argued in the preceding cases.

Some moralists have not suspended favorable judgment on all suicides. Some medievals, weighing the suicides of such as Samson and virgin saints who killed themselves to avoid violation, concluded that the Holy Spirit had inspired their actions. (This, of course, implied the unraised question of whether the Holy Spirit could inspire other suicides.) Henry Davis, in his *Moral and Pastoral Theology*, leaned on the abused distinction between direct and indirect and concluded that a sexually threatened maiden

> may leap from a great height to certain death, for her act has two effects, the first of which is to escape from violation, the second, her death, which is not directly wished but only permitted. The distinction betwen the jump and the fall is obvious. In the case, the maid wishes the jump and puts up with the fall.

Davis' distinction is not obvious to today's moralists who would find the maiden's ability to dissect her intentionality even more remarkable than her passion for material chastity.

Some modern moralists have defended the suicide of a spy who, when captured, could be induced by chemicals or by torture to reveal damaging data. Less attended to are the social witness type suicides related, for example, to the early phase of the Vietnam war. In assessing the objective morality of the suicide of Roger LaPorte, which first signaled to many in Communist China and Indochina the depth of anti-war feeling in America, our judgment should *at the least* show the kind of reserve that Bonhoeffer brings to limit situations. Of the possibility of other moral suicides, it must be said that there are strong presumptions against them, arising from the experience of grounded hope, from the number of alternatives open to imaginative man and from the effects on the bereaved. However, no one is wise enough to say that those presumptions could not be overridden, unless, of course, that someone is privy to knowledge of all possible circumstances. Realistic ethics requires more modesty than that. Thus, the possibility of objectively moral self-killing is an open question, and it may not be excluded that direct self-killing may be a good moral action, in spite of the strong presumptions against it.

In sum, then, death has lost its medical and moral simplicity. We know it now as a process, not a moment; and we have the means to extend or shorten that process. In the older ethics of dying, begged questions reigned unchallenged. The ordinary/extraordinary means rubric is still useful, but not self-sufficient. The borders between ordinary and extraordinary blur and shift, and years ago moralist Gerald Kelly, S.J., pointed out that even ordinary means are not always obligatory. The contention that life could be terminated indirectly and by omission but never directly by commission was not proved—and that is a serious omission.

As Stanford law school dean, Bayless Manning, has said: "The topic as a whole is still subterranean, and decisions are predominantly being made by thousands of doctors in millions of different situations and by undefined, particularized, *ad hoc* criteria." One partial solution to this would be a happily financed, well-managed, hard-working, yearly study-meeting which would bring together doctors, lawyers, moralists of every stripe, insurance experts, nurses, social workers, morticians, sociologists, gravely ill persons, clergymen, journalists, etc., to discuss the current state of dying. The results each year should be energetically publicized in learned journals and in all news media, since death education is needed at every level. (Perhaps some mortal and affluent readers will let their treasures be where their hearts are in this regard.)

Hopefully, a healthier attitude toward death will emerge in our culture. We all could learn from a Donegal Irishman, whose death a few years ago was a testimonial to culture wisdom. While on his deathbed, he was visited by friends who knew, as did he, that this would be their final visit. The dying man ordered his son to bring whisky for the guests.

With this done, the son asked his father if he, too, would indulge. "Oh, no," replied the father with a gentle frown, "I don't want to be meeting the Lord with the smell of the drink on my breath." A few hours later, he died. If we were as at home with death as he, our deliberations on the subject might be more wise.

The Lord of Death and Dying

James M. Sullivan

"Are our means of coping with our finite natures really authentic and mature? Or are they more escapist than genuinely human?" In the age of moon shots and sperm banks, what are we to make of the mystery of death and dying? So asks James M. Sullivan in a piece prompted in part by a visit to Dachau and an encounter with a Lutheran minister who had spent four agonizing years in that concentration camp. The author's answer to such questions makes reference to the death on Calvary and entails a sobering reminder to the Christian community of the hard demands placed upon it. Mr. Sullivan, formery a theological student at Maryknoll, New York, is now engaged in a student overseas program in Hong Kong with the Maryknoll Fathers. He has also been at work on two books, one on the history of mainland China and one on the priesthood. His article is from the Autumn 1971 issue of *Listening*,* a publication of the three theological schools (Roman Catholic, Presbyterian, and Lutheran) that form an ecumenical cluster in Dubuque, Iowa.

I AM WRITING the bulk of this article from Dachau, Germany. Stretched out before me in hideous anti-panorama are the remains of the infamous Nazi concentration camp, where an estimated 31,951 human beings were put to death. I have just talked to a Lutheran minister, himself an inmate of the camp for four years, who now spends his days sharing with visitors to Dachau his experiences of just what it was like to be imprisoned here. When I asked the minister what motivated him to relive, day after day, for

* 2570 Asbury St., Dubuque, Iowa, 52001.

total strangers, the obviously painful experiences of Dachau, I had already anticipated an answer. I had expected him to say something like: "So that this monstrous happening may never happen again"; or "So that we may never forget the evil as well as the good that man is capable of." But although I had seen these responses written elsewhere in the camp museum, the minister gave a more puzzling and perhaps more profound answer. He said that he relives his experiences everyday with visitors to Dachau so that people will realize and appreciate the mystery of death and dying.

How strange! Surely there are lessons to be learned from Dachau. But I had always thought they were political lessons. As far as "religious" lessons go, I have regarded Dachau as a religious embarrassment. It was in that category of reality that has remained elusive: why suffering and death are allowed to exist under the eye of a supposedly loving and merciful God. We have formulated our religious answers, of course; but none of them seemed, for me anyway, to capture the actual horror the human condition can be afflicted with. Or perhaps the answers have been formulated out of a deep sense of the horror, but with faltering interpretations of the real significance of suffering and death. The cross continues to be as big a stumbling block for us as it was for the ancient Jews and Gentiles.

After reflection and study, however, it seems that the minister of Dachau has penetrated deeply into a religious lesson that is at the heart of all human reality: the mystery of death and dying.

Death is absence. And modern man is just not disposed to the acceptance of absence in his life. He is pulsing with activity, life, betterment, even thoughts of eventual self-perfection. Events like Dachau are sad, inexplicable reminders of his negative potentialities, and modern man does not want to be reminded, much less told, that such reality is central to his understanding of life. Men of today feel uncomfortable contradictions between what they strive toward and the evil they know they are equally capable of perpetrating. We would rather not face such contradictions, or our own condition of absence and death.

Crucifixion, death, and suffering, however, are not a goal, an absolute to be striven for. Rather, the critical point is that death, as contemporary existential philosophers and theologians have realized, is the *key*, the all-important means of attaining fulfilment, resurrection, and authentic existence. When we bypass this crucial means, searching for life separate and apart from death, we only court illusion and disaster. The shallow optimism of nineteenth-century Liberalism in religion is a classic example of this. But, as if in ignorance of such historical lessons, we experience the same pitfalls today as we seek to ignore, deny, or escape the all-pervasive fact of death and absence in our lives. We have made idols of ourselves and surrounded ourselves with self-manufactured reminders that man is truly immortal. And deep within ourselves we are deathly afraid because we know we are not. The fact of death continually comes back to haunt us, causing us to live in doubt—regardless of how hard we try to hide our fear. And as such, death controls us: the ultimate irony for us who have thought that we hold ultimate control of our destinies.

It is the person who has faced death, absence, and nothingness, in all the naked horror of what it can mean, who opens for himself the door to resurrection and builds the solid foundation for a meaningful and positive existence. Jesus did this consummately. He faced and suffered hideous torture and death—and appreciated a glorious resurrection—the only authentic resurrection possible, the one wrought through the valley of death. St. Paul described what this means for followers of the Lord: "Where is death's victory?" he asks. "Where is its sting?" Indeed, death does not lose its terror. But precisely because it was faced in all its terror, the man confronting it now has control over it. In a scene from the rock-opera *Jesus Christ Superstar*, Jesus reflects on his own humanity and concludes, "To conquer death you only have to die."

As with all gospel principles, this is as psychologically sound as it is religiously insightful. We mature as human beings and as Christians by squarely facing the death-in-life which is part of all our lives.

In the Year of Our Lord

The year 1971 has brought us to the brink of man's highest technological accomplishment: America's walks on the moon are becoming commonplace, and rock samples are giving us clues to the four and a half billion-year-old origin of the universe. A U.S. presidential proposal has asked Congress to increase its budget by $100 million toward finding a cure for cancer, while new mobility is being given to quadriplegics who can now operate wheelchairs through eye control. A newly discovered technique of applying alpha-wave training promises to be a boon to psychiatrists in their helping of the disturbed. In Indianapolis the members of a newly designed 4-H Club, where one-third of the 16,000 youngsters are poor, black, or both, experience self-discovery and a sense of community responsibility. A midwestern university has undertaken a dual-reform by meeting the environmental crisis as curriculum and doing it through educational redesign as a "communiversity." For a $45 deposit and a $12 storage fee, men can now have their sperm frozen and preserved indefinitely for future insemination. And while such life possibilities are made real here on earth, the newly found science of astrochemistry explores the distinct possibility of finding intelligent life in other parts of the universe.

But is it a coincidence that 1971 has also been afflicted with widespread anxiety, alienation, and a general malaise regarding human values? In South America mothers sell their babies to support the children they already have. It was recently revealed that one hospital bed in four is occupied by a patient whose illness was caused by polluted water. In northeastern Brazil, one of every four children does not live long enough to learn how to walk, while in the United States, $400,000,000 a year is spent on headache remedies. A radio station in Boston holds a pre-Thanksgiving raffle—two turkeys, "one for your table and one for your garbage." And more people, we are told, have spent more time watching and listening to Johnny Carson than to any other human being in history.

And why? Why the escape, why the neglect, why the sham? What causes each of us, in his own way, to avoid confrontation with the absent and seek instead our isolated "clean, well-lighted places"? The pain, the death, the limitation of our humanity are too frightening, too real. And as the poet said, "Humankind cannot bear very much reality."

On the other hand, mankind may be able to bear more reality than it is given credit for—as Jesus proved so tremendously and as the Dachau minister continues to prove today.

In an appendix to his book *Death, Grief, and Mourning,* Lionel Rubinoff titles a section: "The Pornography of Death." It is a most fitting title. For as Rubinoff explains, the subject of death itself has become "pornographic" in modern society: "In the 20th century . . . there seems to have been an unremarkable shift in prudery; whereas copulation has become more and more 'mentionable,' particularly in the Anglo-Saxon societies, death has become more and more 'unmentionable' *as a natural process.*" And, of course, repression often results in obsession. "If we make death unmentionable in polite society—'not before children'—we almost insure the continuation of the 'horror comic,' " Rubinoff concludes.

Robert J. Lifton, who has done extensive research in the area of man's dealing (or nondealing) with death, has written about the "immortality games" he finds people playing among themselves to avoid confronting death. Watching violence on television, for instance, is a prime example of how men can purge themselves of their feelings toward death. On television we can watch it happening to others, fictionalized, glamorized, and far removed from ourselves. In short, the violence of television lets a man feel he has control over death and suffering—a control he so desperately wants, but which perhaps he has not even begun to approach authentically in his own life.[1]

And what of the "immortality games" peculiar to the Church? In Christ, the Church has been given the clearest example of what facing death involves. Ironically, the Church has ignored at many points in her history the critical example of Jesus in this regard. With the Church's emphasis on all that is "present," we have perhaps fallen into the same trap which haunts modern man in general. The Church has not yet realized that the critical means leading to authentically Christian existence are to be found in the crucible of absence. In many ways, this real genius of the Judaeo-Christian mystery has been explored only at certain intervals or by particular individuals throughout history.

Immortality itself is a belief in the "present," but not in the escapist sense of calling men "beyond" death or "away from" death. It rather calls us into a *confrontation* with death. Again referring to the work of Lifton, we find that historically men have always formulated ways of "maintaining a sense of immortality in the face of biological death." Living on through one's sons and daughters; a belief in life after death; immortality through art, invention, and other creative works; being survived by nature itself; the quest and experience of mysticism: all are major ways, Lifton notes, of man's compelling and universal urge to maintain a sense of immortality. All of these modes are to be found very clearly within the Church, as it reflects the history of man himself. And yet again the question haunts us: Are our means of coping with our finite natures really authentic and mature? Or are they more escapist than genuinely human?

Was Jesus a Failure?

Let us look again at the answer given in the life and death of Jesus Christ. What are the undeniably striking facts? First, we have no record that Jesus himself was the father of any children who would go on to bear his name. Secondly, he died at an early age. Both of these facts, in the Jewish mentality especially, rendered his death embarrassingly worthless. For both progeny and long life were the clearest signs for the Jews of favor by God and of a life well-lived. Thirdly, since Jesus was fully human, he certainly realized a potentially terrifying finality to his death (notwithstanding later theological gospel interpretations). Fourthly, he left behind no literature, invention, or work of art. Jesus preached the Kingdom. The Church, which is not synonymous with the Kingdom, was the later creation of the Spirit and the disciples of Jesus. Therefore, Jesus died without thoughts of having founded a mighty and enduring institution, but died rather with a sense of loss, failure, and a lack of any real accomplishment. Finally, consider the death of Jesus itself. He died a shameful death as a criminal. As far as anyone could tell, if he left any heritage, it was one of shame and heartbreak. He died alone and abandoned. He died a cruel, hideous death by crucifixion; and by way of ultimate irony, it was in his time a common death. Not exceptional or striking—just common.

What can we make of this? The death on Calvary and the deaths at Dachau and yesterday's death of a policeman or tomorrow's death of a student all bear a remarkable, almost unbearable similarity. These deaths call us back from the immortality games and shallow plateaus of half-life on which we struggle to exist. And they focus our eyes on the roots of our human existence. They offer us the answer to a question we have been too frightened to ask. They quote us the price with which authentic existence is purchased. We are in a position here to learn much, both individually and as a community.

As individuals, we are given a new perspective on the importance of love and service within the Church and the world, and an appreciation of its implications. The risk of personal security and complacency becomes critical. We grow up as we learn to accept and mature through the experiences of death involved in sharing and sacrificing ourselves in human relationship. Death, like all relationship, is full of ambiguity and uncertainty. It demands more faith and trust than we can calculate and set exacting limits to. In friendship, for example, a death is demanded of the individuals who are willing to risk and to sacrifice for each other. The resurrection of their love, the permanent, the visible, the calculable, is an absolute attained only through an appreciation of the real death involved first.

We mature individually through an acceptance of the inevitable, not only of our own death, but the deaths of those we love and value. We face crises, cruel and difficult as they may be, and learn what it means to live in the realm of reality. Those who struggle to face death learn that there are far easier ways to get around painful experiences, but none more honest or ultimately rewarding. We can try, for example, to put the pain of death out of our minds. We can refuse to look at it, talk about it, cry about it. Instead we build pretty monuments over graves and in our minds. But honest people know that death is too strong and too fundamental a reality to be ignored or glossed over. And no genuine hold on life, just as no genuine resurrection, is attained without a direct confrontation with this reality.

Moreover, as we have indicated earlier, we cannot limit ourselves to actual biological death as the key to life itself. The experiences of death in loneliness, failure, sickness, sadness, and disappointment are just as significant. No logical argument can be set forth to make them sound appealing. Nor should we search for such an argument. The experiences must be endured. The alternative is nonreality, nonlife.

Finally, from the viewpoint of the individual, we note the importance of accepting human limitation. In the age of moon shots and sperm banks it is difficult to conceive of man in terms of limitation. Yet those who fail to do so, history tells us, are those who become the most limited and controlled of all. The eventual self-perfectibility of mankind has always been an attractive theory. But it has also been a deceptive one. Its idolatry, no matter how disguised, builds on false confidence. The Psalms pose this as a recurrent theme: Remember, man, just who you are. It is in that humblest hour of admission to this Word that man gains the strength and confidence to change his world, and cloudy optimism gives way to the solid earth of honest human reality.

A Martyr's Legacy

And what does death mean when applied to the Christian community as a whole? Surely no one is more qualified to answer this than Dietrich Bonhoeffer, a Christian martyr under Nazi rule. Bonhoeffer had some very exacting thoughts on what confronting death means for the Church. And he sacrificed his own life to imprisonment and death as an example of what this could involve for the entire Church. In short, the Church can only be called into resurrection after literally dying in the pattern of her Lord.

During the period of Nazi terror and even today, there was and continues to be widespread debate over whether or not the German clergy should have taken a stand against the government. Some point out that, had they done so, the visible Church most surely would have been extinguished. Bonhoeffer agrees with this, but unlike his opponents, he views the demise positively. Yes, he says, those Church leaders should have stood up in adamant, vocal opposition to the Nazi party in Germany. In such times of crisis, he contends, the individual as well as the community has no recourse but death. To live, at this point, becomes cheap and inauthentic. As a critical sign of faith, we choose death as the only means to real life. Like Christ, the community which strives to be worthy of his name takes the ultimate risk. The Church risks its own extinction in order to remain true to its Lord. It is a frighteningly radical demand. It is faith put to its ultimate test. Yet some would say that the faith which is here manifested is the only kind of faith worth anything. The seed falls into the ground—and dies.

Bonhoeffer's Christianity rebels at any political affiliation. For it has been realized, in the words of Rosemary Ruether, that "the main culprit in the demise of early revolutionary Christianity was the coalescing of Church and society."[2] The Christian community is an independent critic of government, of science, of itself, and of life in general. It is servant—and it is free. From Vietnam to Sundays at the White House to self-made, vitalistic Huxleyan utopias, the confessing Christian risks a stern admonition in the name of the Lord of death and dying. We are not so far removed from the German situation of the 1940s or models like Dietrich Bonhoeffer when an Anglican dean can be imprisoned (January, 1971) in South Africa for vocal criticism of apartheid practices. Nor should we be surprised when we find the real vitality of Christianity crying out through the walls of Connecticut, Missouri, and New York prisons. Or need we be reminded of the everyday deaths involved in the quest for decency and human dignity?

The House of God

How strange, or perhaps very consistent it is that the greatest opposition arising against a Christianity which seeks authentic life through the valley of death and suffering, should come from within institutionalized religion itself. For there is much to be lost in terms of material comforts, large and impressive church memberships, physical and commercial indications of success: everything the "world" considers important. But to opt for these is to choose death of a different sort.

To the confessing Christian, everything points to resurrection. Life is the absolute. But in that great mystery of Christianity, the journey to Life is routed through the heart of humanity and an acceptance of certain death.

The final words spoken to me by the Dachau minister reflect the paradox as well as the all-important key to what we are reflecting upon here. The meaning of his life, the minister told me, and the key to what kept him and his fellow clergymen alive during those years of agony in Dachau, were the simple, mysterious words of the Bible: "How awesome is this place! This is none other than the house of God" (Gen. 28:17).

Notes

1. See R. J. Lifton, "The Politics of Immortality," *Psychology Today* (November, 1970).
2. See *The Radical Kingdom* (New York: Harper & Row, 1970).

Appendix: Reflections on This Venture, after Ten Years

This tenth anniversary issue provides an occasion for looking backward. The concept of *New Theology* was born almost in an instant of conversation in the office of Clement Alexandre of Macmillan one morning in 1962. There seemed to be so much excitement in the theological world, but so little of it was accessible to people who were not near major periodical collections. Would we be willing to risk the task of anthologizing articles that most impressed us? Such a task involved a great deal of consulting, hunch-playing, listening, interviewing, reading, risk-taking. We are not sure we knew what we were getting into, but Mr. Alexandre was encouraging and helpful, as have been so many other people. The reviews and the many citations in footnotes of other peoples' writings have since led us to believe that *New Theology* has come to be regarded as a rather faithful record, a delineator, or at least a monitor of tendencies in religious thought.

The occasional critics of the concept have argued that the series may have contributed to the passion for novelty and even the faddism that came to characterize so much of the thought of the 1960s and that eventually may have led many people to turn from theology. We can see why those who read only the numbered titles of these books might think that such would be the case, but those who read the introductions and the selections will have noticed, we hope, that the editors have consistently been concerned to trace continuity as much as change. Whenever possible, we chose articles that self-consciously related to long traditions of thought. It has seemed to us that whereas the themes and accents have changed, there have been basically two main strands in the past ten years of upheaval. One has represented the attempt to make theology an earthbound, secular, almost humanistic preoccupation. The other dealt with what Peter Berger once called "signals of transcendence," and signified the attempt to find new bases for God-talk and metaphysics.

Neither of us believes that systematic theology is today in a particularly healthy state. We have not shared the glee of many who once happily said good-bye to the great twentieth-century voices associated with Catholic and Protestant biblical, liturgical, ecumenical, or "neoorthodox" theology—especially since so few of the rejoicers have contributed much to a replacement. We seem to be in a moment when religious experience is being newly valued, when the narrative of religious communities is being told once again. No doubt, the day will come when the interpreters of personal experience and community will again find appropriate language and form. Whether that moment will come soon enough to warrant another decade of *New Theology* is a question we are reluctant to answer at this time. The chances are that we may turn our attention to other projects, not because there is a shortage of worthwhile material—we hope numbers 8, 9, and 10 have been as vital as numbers 1, 2, and 3—but because nothing should last forever, because no institutions should be unquestioned and self-reproducing without reflection.

Whether or not there will be more books in this series, we feel that we should take particular note once more of the many journal editors who made our work easy by their preselective endeavors. They are the ones who first had to make judgments on the merits of publishing the scores of articles that we reproduced. They take their work very seriously; with few resources and crammed schedules, they were consistently generous to us.

After a decade we also totted up a few scores and wish to pay special honor to a few periodicals that made repeated appearances here. *Theology Today*, *Union Seminary Quarterly Review*, and *The Commonweal* each made eight appearances. (We like to think that diffidence and the assumption that our readers were subscribers to *The Christian Century* helped restrain us to the point that only three times did we reprint material from the journal with which we are associated.) *Continuum,* no longer among us, was the source six times; the *Canadian Journal of Theology* and *Religion in Life* provided four articles each. The other three-timers have been the *Scottish Journal of Theology, Theological Studies, Interpretation,* and the *Journal of Religion.* Since we tried to read all the major journals of the English-speaking theological world, we must pay tribute to the editors of those journals that repeatedly printed what struck us as apropos works of first quality.

While the accent has been on Christian thought, five Jewish journals provided articles; the Christianity has been generally Western. Only once was an Eastern Orthodox review drawn upon. We set out to monitor the English-speaking press, but eight times also reached for the Continent; the British Isles were represented by eleven different journals and Canada by one. Six secular, twelve academically based, fourteen ecumenical-general-nondenominational religious, six Protestant denominational, and twelve Roman Catholic journals round out the list.

Although our main negotiations have been with publishers, the authors have had to be cooperative, too, since many of them held the copyright and all of them had to be pestered for permission. We are happy to say that they have been almost uniformly generous, and we acknowledge our debt to them, for without them we could only have printed introductions and published white space.

Future historians of theology, we are confident, will be talking about the people whose writings have appeared here. A few of the century's titans have been represented: Karl Barth, Mircea Eliade, Bernard Lonergan, S.J. Continental comers and arrivers included Wolfhart Pannenberg and Jürgen Moltmann, Johannes Metz and Roger Garaudy, Heinrich Ott and Eduard Schweizer, Hans-Werner Bartsch and

Jan Lochman; from England, people like John Macquarrie and David Jenkins graced the pages. There have been literary types, among them Walter Ong, S.J., John Moffitt, and Tom Driver; church historians were Sidney E. Mead, Sydney Ahlstrom, Albert Outler; biblical scholars included Joseph Cahill and Krister Stendahl.

Vincent Harding, Preston N. Williams, and others represented black religion; and Emil Fackenheim led a cast of Jewish thinkers. Women have been well represented, among them Irene Marinoff, Daphne Nash, M. Romanus Penrose, Jeanne Richie, Rosemary Ruether, and Rachel Conrad Wahlberg; among lay theologians were William Stringfellow, Michael Novak, and Daniel Callahan. Names associated with conservatism appeared regularly: Kenneth Hamilton and R. P. C. Hanson are typical.

Much of the theological debate of the decade occurred between innovative "mainstreamers" and those styled "radical." In the former camp we would list John B. Cobb, Jr., Langdon Gilkey, James M. Gustafson, Gordon Kaufman, Carl Braaten, Herbert Richardson, Robert McAfee Brown, Avery Dulles, Paul Ramsey, and many others. The radical camp would include Richard Rubenstein and Harvey Cox, Sam Keen and Leslie Dewart, Daniel Berrigan—way back then, already—and Richard Shaull. But we are only scratching the surface, and there are scores more. It has always given us pleasure to see that earlier volumes in the series sell and circulate almost as well as later volumes, a sign that the people we have just cited and their colleagues remain subjects of interest (or authors on subjects of interest) to people year after year.

The editing represents moonlighting in the *Christian Century* offices, too. We like to think of it as an extension of that weekly magazine's influence, for without the vantage gained there—amid press releases, news stories, article after article—neither of us would have had the credentials to do any selecting. Three editors have headed the magazine during these years: the late Kyle Haselden, Alan Geyer, and now James M.

Wall. We thank them for encouraging or winking at this operation, while keeping their own pressure of deadlines on us. Most of all, we acknowledge the decade-long faithful service, correspondence, editorial work, and attention to detail on the part of Joanne Younggren. We love her.

M. E. M. and D. G. P.

New Theology No. 1

New Theology No. 2

New Theology No. 3

New Theology No. 4

New Theology No. 5

New Theology No. 6

New Theology No. 7